AMERICAN COUNCIL ON EDUCATION

CELEBRATING 100 YEARS

Sundial located at the site of the first
Ohio University building, erected in 1807.

AMERICAN COUNCIL ON EDUCATION

CELEBRATING 100 YEARS

GREENWICH
PUBLISHING

Georgia State University commencement, 2012

CONTENTS

Introduction 13

Part One: Educating the Nation 18

Part Two: Expansion, Legislation, and Inclusion 41

Part Three: Fostering Equity and Change 68

Part Four: Advocacy, Access, and Internationalization 93

Timeline 134

Underclassmen at the University of Mary Washington (VA)
(then Mary Washington College), circa 1980s

Students working in a lab at George Mason University (VA), 1964.

A "farmerette," the nickname given to Vassar College (NY) students who worked as agricultural laborers in the summer months of World War I and World War II.

Roanoke College (VA) Administration Building, 2015.

Introduction

T ake an early morning walk on many college campuses—before the students stream in, before the day starts—and you can easily picture the typical college or university in the early years of the twentieth century: commanding brick buildings, the immaculate stretch of lawn, quiet permeating the halls. It is an idyllic scene, but one that held little promise for much of the population at the time and made only a narrow, though powerful, impact on the country as a whole. Today, among the sophisticated research labs, profusion of technology, and soaring, light-filled contemporary architecture, you can see a group of people who want to transform American higher education into something different: something more public-minded, more inclusive, more democratic.

War was the catalyst for the major changes in higher education in the 1900s, as is often the case with major social transformations. The founding of the American Council on Education was closely connected to World War I, when representatives from four higher education associations began discussions on how American higher education could contribute to the national war effort. They were joined

Commemorative tin featuring the ACE seal, which includes three torches (the "lights of learning") and seven stars (the original liberal arts of grammar, rhetoric, dialectics, arithmetic, geometry, astronomy, and music).

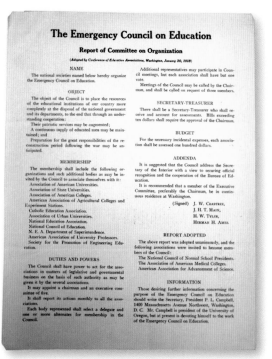

First official document of the Emergency Council on Education, January 30, 1918.

by other higher education leaders to create the Emergency Council on Education in the early months of 1918, renamed the American Council on Education—ACE—in July of that year.

Browsing the 2,700-odd boxes of archived ACE papers and other material at Stanford University (CA), it is clear to see the hard work, painstaking processes, carefully managed relationships, and deep care that helped ACE thrive in the early years. Over the decades, ACE's mission expanded into serving as the major coordinating body for U.S. higher education institutions, spearheading programs, advocating for legislation, conducting research, and undertaking initiatives that have helped form the postsecondary landscape in the United States. The Council also has been an unflagging advocate for expanding the higher education leadership pipeline to underrepresented groups and for easing the path to a degree for post-traditional students, people of color, women, and members of the military and veterans.

Higher education was at a critical turning point in 1918, and we find ourselves at another crossroads in 2018. There is still work to do. As we look toward the next 100 years, we envision mission-driven, innovative, and financially resilient colleges and universities providing a quality and affordable higher education to a diverse group of learners who will transform and lead their local communities, a thriving nation, and a globalizing world. As a community, we can look to a number of strategies to promote change for the twenty-first century, such as reimagining diversity and equity for students, faculty, and leaders; enabling the expansion of flexible completion pathways; developing innovative institutions and leaders that are learner-centered, outcome focused, and globally engaged; and fostering effective public policy reform based on expertise, evidence, and engagement.

Our success depends on us all: college presidents and other senior leaders, faculty, public policymakers, business leaders, philanthropic organizations, and students themselves. ACE will be there to work hand in hand with you—a partnership that has seen a century of progress and holds the promise of the future for all of higher education.

Ted Mitchell, ACE President

"To stimulate discussion, to focus opinion, and in the end to bring about joint action on major matters of higher educational policy—these are the things that the American Council on Education was created to do."

—Samuel P. Capen, ACE President (1919–1922), 1921

Lawrence Technological University (MI)
commencement, 1956.

PART ONE

Educating the Nation

(1918–1945)

The American Council on Education (ACE) was founded in 1918 in response to a national military emergency. Although conscription had supplied the U.S. armed forces with 2.8 million foot soldiers to fight in World War I, there was a dire shortage of educated, trained field officers to lead them.

In January 1918 in the nation's capital, representatives from 14 higher education associations officially formed the Emergency Council on Education. They soon changed the name to the American Council on Education and appointed Donald J. Cowling, the head of the Association of American Colleges and president of Carlton College (MN), to be the

Student Army Training Corps, Alma College (MI), 1918.

Homecoming parade for soldiers returning from World War I, Augustana College (IL), 1919.

WELCOME HOME
OUR HEROES

WELCOME

Samuel P. Capen in his office in Hayes Hall at the University of Buffalo, circa 1920s.

The Educational Record

Published Quarterly by

The American Council on Education

| Volume 1 | January, 1920 | No. 1 |

Editor:

SAMUEL PAUL CAPEN

CONTENTS

Educational Bills Before Congress
By the Editor

The American Council on Education
By the Editor

Annual Subscription, $2.00

The first issue of ACE's quarterly journal,
The Educational Record.

first president. Despite the name change, the Council's aim remained the same: to coordinate the resources of higher education to meet the nation's immediate wartime needs. This included intensive training of officers and key personnel in various technical, vocational, and military subjects. In addition, faculty research programs were deemed essential to exploring warfare inventions and innovations.

One of the Council's first tasks was to survey the nation's higher education campuses to identify those best suited to fulfill the specialized training needs of the U.S. Army and U.S. War and State Departments. To ensure the military would have an ongoing supply of trained leadership personnel, ACE Chairman Samuel P. Capen helped expand the nascent Army Reserve Officers' Training Corps (ROTC), authorized by President Woodrow Wilson's National Defense Act (1916). Capen, a former higher education specialist at the U.S. Bureau of Education who would become ACE's second president, helped grow the ROTC from 35,000 college-level enrollees in 1916 to 120,000 by 1925. He also established *The Educational Record*, a quarterly journal that published scholarly articles on how to best link higher education with the nation's interests.

Like ACE, other organizations formed in response to the crisis of World War I. In 1916, the National Research Council (NRC) burgeoned from the prominent National Academy of Sciences. NRC served to coordinate scientific research and increase scientific contributions to the nation's war efforts. Although established in a time of national emergency, both ACE and NRC proved their value beyond the war and continue to be a strong presence in their respective fields today.

Rise to National Leadership

After World War I hostilities ended on November 11, 1918, ACE redirected itself to more expansive peacetime roles. Prior to the war, most colleges and universities operated with an independent, autonomous focus. ACE's wartime involvement, however, had helped create a more centralized point of view. Capen reexamined the missions, objectives, and processes of various institutions and helped spearhead a standardized, professional evaluation and accreditation system for institutions of higher learning in the United States.

College women, like the Vassar College (NY) students pictured here, were at the forefront of the suffrage movement in the early twentieth century.

ACE assisted in drafting and adopting criteria that reflected the basic standards of a sound postsecondary education and developed peer evaluation procedures to ensure an institution's academic quality. In 1920, the Council published the first official listing of accredited higher education institutions.

The 1920 ACE standards of accreditation arrived just in time. Enrollment at college and university campuses grew at an accelerated pace in postwar expansion, with the most dramatic increase occurring from 1920 to 1929—a period in which enrollments doubled. Undergraduate programs in business, dominated by male students, and teaching, heavily populated by female students, grew most dramatically. Professional programs in areas including law and health also saw significant growth—nearly 75 percent overall.

The makeup and objectives of the student population had changed as well. Before World War I, college students were predominantly affluent white males pursuing a classical education in the arts or sciences. The new student population was much more diverse, including working-class men—many of whom had participated in military training on college campuses—women, and minorities. Most of these students were first-generation, and they saw their education as a doorway into a career in business or commerce.

"In the future, far more than in the past, the professions will comprise both men and women. . . . The day of studying occupations for women is over."

—Gertrude S. Martin, Chair of the ACE Committee on Training of Women for Professional Service, 1921

Observing the seismic social and academic shifts occurring at its member institutions' campuses, ACE responded in a variety of key ways. In 1920, ACE established the Committee on the Training of Women for Professional Service to raise the status of working women to professional levels. The committee published its research of women in the workplace—the first of its kind—in *The Educational Record* in 1922. In 1927, ACE became the first educational organization to promote standard measures of achievement and potential through psychological exams for high school students and college freshmen. Finally, the Council published *American Universities and Colleges* in 1928. This compendium was the first of its kind, offering extensive information to students, parents, advisors, and educators on all accredited colleges and universities that offered a baccalaureate degree.

An early advertisement for Robert Morris University (PA).

The receptionist's corner of Robert Morris' main corridor.

A section of one of the airy well-lighted shorthand rooms at Robert Morris.

The heart of the Robert Morris Placement Service, which operates with no cost to the student and with no obligation upon the employer. Through this office hundreds of students and graduates are placed every year.

In this section of the Business Science Laboratory, Robert Morris students learn the operation of duplicating and calculating machines.

A Perfect Storm

Although the stock market crash of October 29, 1929, effectively brought the Roaring Twenties to an end, it would take three years of economic hardship before U.S. colleges and universities felt the full impact. By 1932, personal income and payment of taxes had plummeted, effectively reducing state funds to public universities by 40 percent and reducing endowments and financial support to private universities by almost twice as much. U.S. colleges and universities were forced to slash faculty salaries, increase class sizes, freeze new hires, and eliminate perceived "extras" like construction projects, library purchases, travel, and research budgets.

A plaque honoring the women serving in World War II at the University of Rochester (NY).

The 1930s saw drastically decreased education options and labor markets. While the number of high school–age students increased by 2 million between 1930 and 1940, young people had fewer opportunities than ever before. In 1935, ACE organized the American Youth Commission to address the plight of millions of school-age adolescents who were roaming the country hungry, homeless, and searching for work. The commission evaluated youth employment opportunities, unemployment problems, and the actions and responsibilities of various state governments. The commission's report reflected a national shift in the attitude toward the education of children in the United States. For the first time, education had become a national priority, with widespread demand for the federal government to guarantee an educated populace.

In 1938, ACE further advanced efforts for educational equity and access in primary and secondary schools. Dismayed by the disproportionate withdrawal of funding from minority schools, ACE began studying the effects of racism on black children in the United States and published a series of reports on equal opportunity in education. The reports—which included *Children of Bondage: The Personality Development of Negro Youth in the Urban South* by Allison Davis and John Dollard (1940) and *Growing Up in the Black Belt: Negro Youth in the Rural South* by Charles Spurgeon Johnson (1941)—foreshadowed and highlighted the harsh reality of life for black children in the United States prior to the Supreme Court's 1954 *Brown v. Board of Education* ruling that segregation in public schools was unconstitutional.

Advances in Adult, Military, and GI Education

As ACE members grappled with the changes wrought by the Great Depression, they also kept watch on the international conflict escalating in Europe. When the United States officially entered World War II in 1941, the Council was ready to apply the lessons learned from World War I to the next generation of U.S. soldiers.

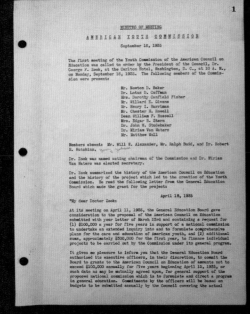

Minutes from the American Youth Commission meeting, September 16, 1935.

An unemployed young man in Washington, DC, 1938.

The hardships endured during the Great Depression created the opportunity—and necessity—to recast the foundation of the educational system in the United States. During the crisis, combined personal income in the United States plummeted by 45 percent and unemployment rose to 25 percent, causing a precipitous drop in the payment of local property taxes, the lifeblood of most educational budgets. Funding to schools was slashed, and the effects were felt in every facet of education: deep cuts to faculty salaries; increases in class sizes; a cessation in expenditures for books, supplies, maintenance, and research; and the near closure of some state universities.

In response, ACE established the American Youth Commission in 1935 and exposed a huge funding gap between the United States' cash-strapped local educational systems and federally funded jobs-oriented New Deal programs. Nearly 4 million teens and young adults were living on the streets, undereducated, and unemployed. The commission lobbied strongly for federal planning and provision for at-risk youth.

The Great Depression precipitated more efficient, standardized, and integrated schools—essentially laying a pipeline for the colleges and universities of the future. The financial crisis meant less funding for schools, which generated innovative solutions. Many geographic areas facing big cuts simply closed minority schools; the city of Philadelphia, for example, combined its student populations to create the nation's first integrated school system. And while schoolbooks had varied widely according to regional preferences, strained Depression-era budgets forced publishers to create the first standardized textbooks.

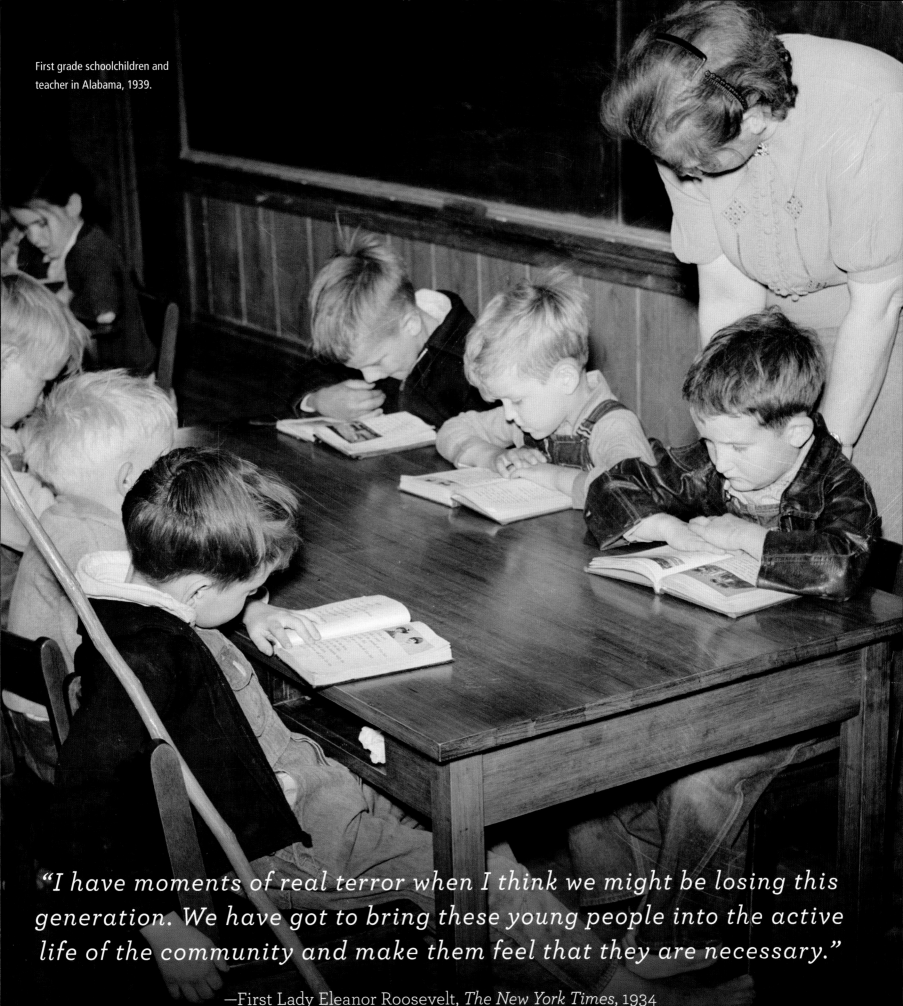

First grade schoolchildren and teacher in Alabama, 1939.

"I have moments of real terror when I think we might be losing this generation. We have got to bring these young people into the active life of the community and make them feel that they are necessary."

—First Lady Eleanor Roosevelt, *The New York Times*, 1934

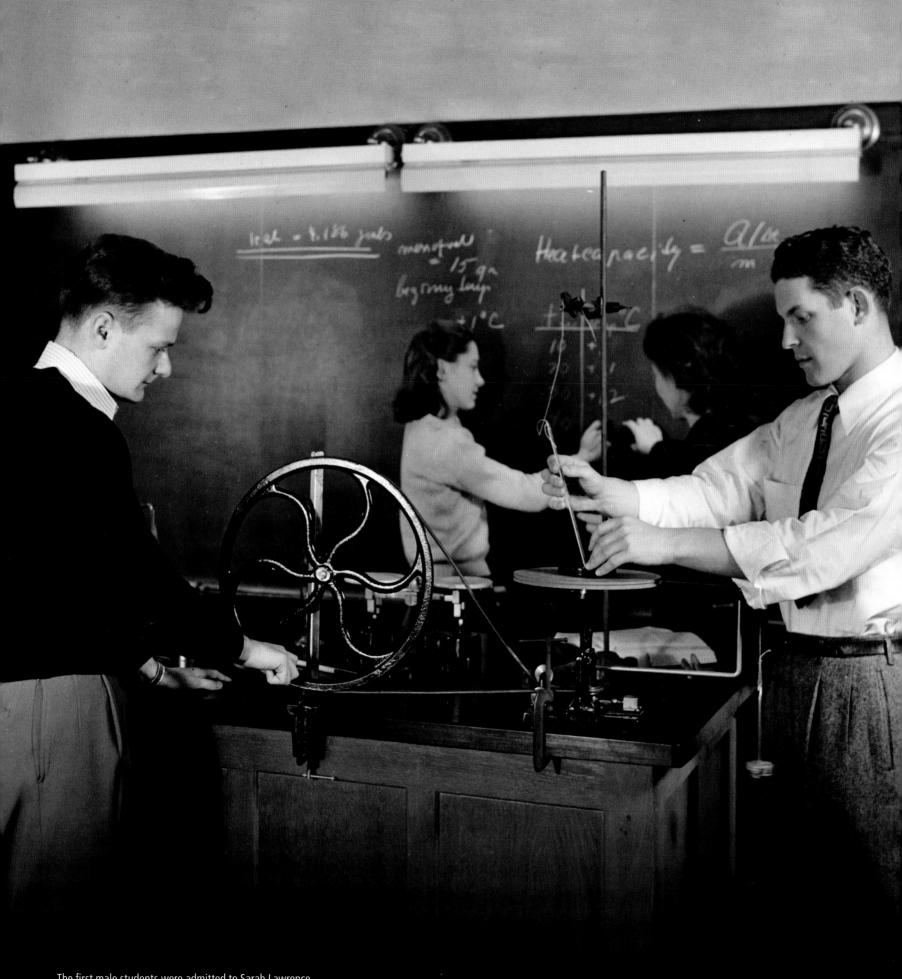

The first male students were admitted to Sarah Lawrence College (NY) under the GI Bill after World War II.

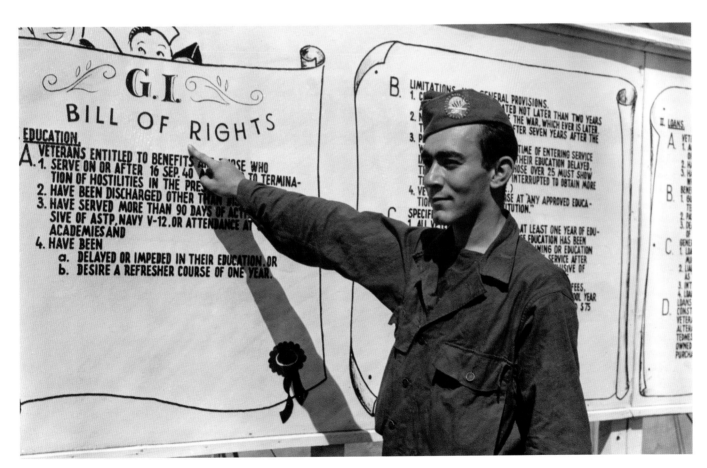

Maryland State Department of Education
GED OFFICE • 200 W. BALTIMORE ST. • BALTIMORE, MD. 21201

The attached High School Diploma has been awarded through your attainment of the following scores on the five General Educational Development Tests.

	WRITING SKILLS	SOCIAL STUDIES	SCIENCE	LITERATURE	MATHEMATICS	TOTAL OF SCORES
TEST SCORE	54	57	63	54	66	294
PERCENTILE RANK	66%	76%	90%	66%	95%	
CERTIFIED	1	2	3	4	5	

MONTH 08 DAY YEAR 48

ROBERT G JENKINS
912 DELRAY DRIVE
FOREST HILL MD 21050

Congratulations on achieving the Maryland Diploma. Opportunities in both business and higher education are now open to you that were previously unobtainable. Your accomplishment should give you a feeling of satisfaction that is certainly shared by the GED Office.

ALWAYS INCLUDE YOUR SOCIAL SECURITY NUMBER IN COMMUNICATION WITH THIS OFFICE

HSE 67106 - 1/83

GED® certificate, awarded in 1948.

ACE led the country in responding to the educational needs of World War II veterans by implementing a series of groundbreaking programs. In 1942, the Council spearheaded the GED® test, a series of standardized exams used to measure a service member's proficiency in science, mathematics, social studies, reading, and writing among those who did not complete high school. That same year, ACE also developed the Military Evaluations Program to accurately award college credit for various military courses and training.

Finally, the Council helped draft and then lobbied for the passage of the Servicemen's Readjustment Act of 1944. Also called the GI Bill, the act provided educational benefits to veterans. President Franklin D. Roosevelt signed the bill into law on June 22, 1944, stating, "[This bill] gives emphatic notice to the men and women in our armed forces that the American people do not intend to let them down." He added, "There is still much to be done."

For many veterans, the GI Bill meant a college education and a solid start in postwar life.

The International Relations Club at
Georgetown College (KY), 1948.

Opposite: Because of a lack of funding following the Great Depression, from 1931 to 1933, students at Weber State University (UT) were allowed to make in-kind tuition payments using homegrown produce and livestock.

Right: Due to the demand for affordable housing caused by the dramatic increase of married students after World War II, Findlay College (OH) created "Trailer City," a community of federally supplied units just feet from the athletic field to house married couples and families. Below: The war prompted curricula such as civil pilot training, like this Navy flight class at Western Illinois University, 1941.

The GED® Test

Draft workers check names and numbers at New York Selective Service headquarters as numbers are drawn in Washington in the nation's first wartime lottery, 1942.

An October 13, 1942, headline foreshadows the deluge of soldiers who would return from the war without a high school diploma.

After the Japanese attack on Pearl Harbor in December 1941, millions of young Americans volunteered for service in the U.S. armed forces. Many left high school and lied about their age to enlist. In 1942, when Congress officially lowered the draft age from 21 to 18, more teenagers, including those who had dropped out of school during the Great Depression, were drafted into service. In fact, the military estimates that more than half of the 16.1 million U.S. service members who served in World War II had not completed high school.

The idea of a "general educational development" test evolved when the U.S. Armed Forces Institute (USAFI) approached ACE for assistance in evaluating veterans. USAFI needed a tool to help colleges, universities, and potential employers determine veterans' educational training and courses while in the military, as well as their ability to handle college-level work. The GED® test was initially based on a battery of nine exams developed by E. F. Lindquist called the Iowa Tests of Educational Development (ITED), which assessed students' abilities in English language arts, social studies, science, and mathematics. While modeled after the ITED, the 1942 GED® test consisted of only five exams.

For the first wave of war veterans returning to the United States, the GED® test proved popular among those who had either failed to complete high school or had mediocre high school academic records. By mid-1943, over 400 colleges and universities had officially endorsed ACE's recommendations for the GED® test and were using veterans' successful completion of the test as the basis for their college admission. The academic achievement of student veterans was documented throughout the 1940s, confirming the validity and value of the program.

For many years, the GED® test was only available to military veterans. In the 1970s, Job Corps, a federal agency assisting high school dropouts, voiced interest in GED® testing for disadvantaged teenagers. (Since 1955, ACE had required a minimum age of 21 to take the test, specifically to discourage teenagers from viewing it as an alternative to high school study.) In 1978, ACE created a

First Lady Barbara Bush at a GED® ceremony, 1989.

second-generation GED® test for 18-year-old civilians to achieve high school equivalency. Successive generations of the GED® test followed in 1988 and 2002.

In 2011, ACE partnered with Pearson, an educational publishing company, to create a groundbreaking joint venture that would drive a new vision for the GED® program. Launched in 2014, this comprehensive program aims to prepare adult learners for today's jobs and for postsecondary education programs. Several colleges now utilize higher-level GED® scores to determine course placement, and some award college credit based on GED® test scores. Today, the United States has more than 3,200 official GED® testing centers operating in adult education centers, community colleges, and public schools.

"Probably no instrument of evaluation in the history of education has been so widely used and accepted as have the tests of General Educational Development."

—Harry E. Tyler, Assistant to the Director for Research, United States Armed Forces Institute, "The GED Tests—Friends or Foes," 1956

Students crowd the cafeteria at Mackenzie Hall after a postwar enrollment boom at Wayne State University (MI) in the mid-1950s.

The GI Bill

Copy of the Servicemen's Readjustment Act (GI Bill) of 1944.

As early as 1942, President Franklin D. Roosevelt appointed a commission—which included ACE President George F. Zook—to help America's World War II veterans return to civilian life. The following year, during his June 28, 1943, radio broadcast fireside chat, President Roosevelt said, "While concentrating on military victory, we are not neglecting the planning of things to come. . . . I have assured our men in the armed forces that the American people would not let them down when the war is won."

Sixteen days after D-Day, on June 22, 1944, Roosevelt signed the Servicemen's Readjustment Act, commonly called the GI Bill, into law. The GI Bill, strongly advocated by ACE and the American Legion, awarded military veterans broad and generous economic rights in three key areas: educational support, unemployment benefits, and loan guarantees. The bill's educational benefits included annual tuition payments of up to $500 for one to four years, depending on age and length of service, plus a monthly stipend for living expenses. Notably, the benefits were awarded to individuals rather than institutions, so veterans could apply them to the college, university, or vocational, technical, or apprentice

President Roosevelt signs the GI Bill in the Oval Office on June 22, 1944.

training of their choice. Fifty-one percent of all veterans, roughly 8 million people, accessed the GI Bill's educational provisions, with about one-fourth pursuing college degrees and the remainder pursuing vocational training.

The bill's unemployment benefits gave those looking for work $20 per week for up to one year. The GI Bill's loan program also gave veterans government-insured credit to access low-interest home, business, and farm loans. Millions of veterans took advantage of these loan opportunities to achieve the American dream of home ownership. New home construction in U.S. suburbs flourished after World War II. In addition, the bill provided veterans with medical care in a national network of newly established veterans-only hospitals.

With few exceptions, the GI Bill significantly improved the nation's social fabric and economic prospects. Higher education was now accessible to the middle class, and the GI Bill helped to produce professionals in areas from engineering to science to teaching to medicine. Many of the nation's postwar leaders were educated on the GI Bill: presidents George H. W. Bush and Gerald Ford; senators Daniel Inouye (D-HI), Robert Dole (R-KS), and John Warner (R-VA); and Supreme Court Chief Justice William Rehnquist and associate justices John Paul Stevens and Byron White. Pulitzer Prize–winning author Frank McCourt remembered in an interview for the PBS documentary series *Only a Teacher*: "When I got out of the army, I had the GI Bill. Since I had no high school education or anything like that, I came to NYU, and they took a chance on me and let me in."

Twenty-one years later, in 1965, the deputy director of the Veterans Administration reported that the 1944 GI Bill had more than paid for itself. V. R. Cardozier summarized in *Colleges and Universities in World War II* (1993): "The increased income of college graduates educated under the GI Bill resulted in increased tax payments that exceeded the expenditures of their education. Increased income resulted in greater purchasing power and a larger market for goods and services produced by the American economy, thereby providing more and better jobs. Perhaps even more important overall was the improvement in quality of life."

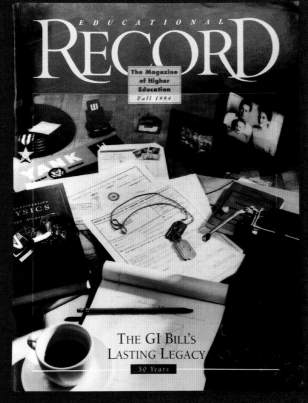

The fall 1994 issue of *The Educational Record*, celebrating 50 years of the GI Bill.

Hundreds of servicemen enrolled in Grove City College's (PA) war training programs during World War II. By the time the war ended, more than 4,000 servicemen had attended the different training programs at Grove City.

"With the signing of this bill a well-rounded program of special veterans' benefits is nearly completed. It gives emphatic notice to the men and women in our armed forces that the American people do not intend to let them down."

—President Franklin D. Roosevelt, statement on signing the GI Bill, June 22, 1944

West Virginia University students at the card

PART TWO

Expansion, Legislation, and Inclusion

(1946–1973)

From coordinating leadership training of U.S. military personnel in the early days of World War I to helping to draft the Servicemen's Readjustment Act of 1944 (the GI Bill), the American Council on Education (ACE) figured prominently in advancing higher education through both world wars and the Great Depression. As a result of these efforts, student bodies at colleges and universities in the United States became more diverse in race, ethnicity, religion, gender, and economic background.

Students at Vassar College (NY) in class after World War II, before the college became coed in 1969.

Maryland State College (now the University of Maryland Eastern Shore) golf team, 1961–62.

These successes in ACE's first 25 years quickly became stepping-stones to many more achievements. After World War II, the Council worked with President Truman to create a commission to evaluate and recommend ways to improve the higher education system in the United States. It also elevated higher education standards to ensure the United States could compete on the world stage and standardized higher education testing nationwide. In the late 1960s and early 1970s, ACE led efforts to increase access to financial aid for all students and to provide equal access to education for minority students and female students.

Indeed, ACE's initiatives from 1946 to 1973 would allow more Americans entrée to higher education than ever before.

The Black Student Association at the University of Memphis (TN), 1972–73.

Montgomery College (then Montgomery Junior College) reading room, 1964.

"It is expected that the . . . growth in college enrollment during the next decade will be absorbed by the community colleges. The community-centered, community-serving institution is rapidly emerging as a distinctive American institution."

—George F. Zook, ACE President (1934–1950) and Chairman, President's Commission on Higher Education,

ACE's second headquarters on Massachusetts Avenue in Washington, DC.

Portrait of ACE President George F. Zook.

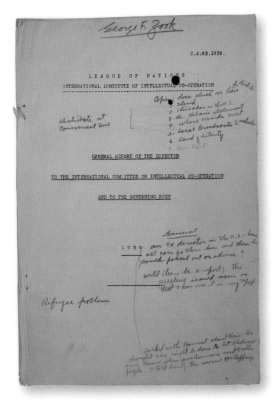

George F. Zook's notes from the 1939 League of Nations International Institute of Intellectual Co-operation.

A Fuller Realization of Democracy

In 1946, President Harry Truman asked ACE President George F. Zook to chair the 28-member Presidential Commission on Higher Education. Truman charged the panel to reexamine the United States' system of colleges and universities "in terms of its objectives, methods, and facilities; and in the light of the social role it has to play."

The Truman Commission, often called the Zook Commission, was historically significant: it was the first time a U.S. president had asked for a national look at higher education, an area previously left to local and state governments. With this commission, the federal government was poised to take an active role in broadening the concept of democracy both domestically and overseas. Under Zook's leadership, the commission delivered a six-volume report, *Higher Education for American Democracy*, in 1947. Each volume addressed specific issues and recommended changes for a better, more attainable and inclusive system of higher education.

The report contended (as evidenced by the success of student veterans) that given opportunity and support, any student who had the drive and motivation to pursue higher education could succeed if certain barriers were removed. Among the barriers cited were college quotas that denied admission to all but a very restricted number of racial, religious, or handicapped minorities; the cost of tuition and college expenses; and the geographical availability of college to those in need of more local options.

Volume II of the report, titled *Equalizing and Expanding Educational Opportunity*, recommended eliminating quotas as well as expanding the number of tuition-free community colleges across the country. It called for open transfer policies for community college students pursuing a four-year degree and suggested extensive increases in federal aid for students who needed assistance paying college tuition as well as day-to-day expenses.

Not all the Zook Commission recommendations were well-received: barriers for minority college admissions would remain for another two decades and a caucus of Southern legislators would block broad funding of color-blind student aid. However, the subsequent nationwide expansion of the community college system represented a historic turning point. As Ordway Tead, chair of the New York Board of Higher Education, wrote, "Whatever its numerous faults and deficiencies, this report will historically come to be acknowledged as supplying something of a landmark, something of a symbol of the end of one era and the beginning of another."

True to President Truman's original vision, the United States would, as stated in the report, embrace "higher education for a fuller realization of democracy in every phase of living."

International Scope and Nationwide Standards

In addition to working on President Truman's Presidential Commission on Higher Education, in 1946 ACE lent pivotal support to the creation and passage of Senator J. William Fulbright's scholarship program, intended to advance mutual understanding of U.S. democracy both at home and overseas. Later that year, at President Truman's urging, ACE also helped establish the United Nations Educational, Scientific and Cultural Organization (UNESCO), which provides international exchange opportunities for American scholars and administrators.

As educational opportunities expanded, the three organizations responsible for testing student readiness for enrollment at various higher education levels joined to form the Educational Testing Service (ETS). Founded in 1947 by ACE, the Carnegie Foundation for the Advancement of Teaching, and the College Entrance Examination Board, ETS was designed to streamline the educational assessment process. It soon became the nation's leading nonprofit purveyor of key standardized tests and exams, including Advanced Placement (AP), the Scholastic Assessment Test (SAT), the College Level Examination Program (CLEP), the National Teacher Examination, and the Graduate Record Examinations (GRE). Today, ETS develops, administers, and scores more than 50 million assessment tests each year at more than 9,000 locations worldwide.

U.S. marshals accompany the first African American student, James Meredith, to class at the University of Mississippi, 1962.

Opening a New Door to Education

While ACE promoted standardization, the Council also continued to advance educational equality and access for students of diverse backgrounds. In 1949, it released a survey of college admission practices titled *On Getting Into College*. The report found widespread admission discrimination against black, Jewish, and Catholic students. ACE led the cause for educational equality by publishing additional studies and reports into the next decade. In 1954, national widespread, persistent efforts to end discrimination in educational settings culminated in a milestone victory in the Supreme Court's ruling in *Brown v. Board of Education*.

Well aware that *Brown v. Board of Education* would not completely eliminate such discrimination, ACE continued to promote educational equality. In 1962, ACE formed the Committee on Equality of Educational Opportunity in the wake of issues that were raised during the integration of the University of Mississippi. Two years later, ACE established the Office of Urban Affairs, which evolved into the Office of Minorities in Higher Education.

Four-time All-American basketball player Henry Logan, the first African American athlete at Western Carolina University and the first African American athlete to compete at any predominantly white public institution in North Carolina, 1965.

In 1964, President Lyndon Johnson asked ACE to assist in crafting language and policy for a landmark piece of legislation to expand federal aid to all qualified students seeking higher education. The Higher Education Act of 1965 was as sweeping in vision and scope as the 1944 GI Bill. As President Johnson announced upon signing it into law, it was the legislative key to opening "a new door for the young people of America . . . the most important door that will ever open—the door to education."

"So to thousands of young people education will be available. And it is a truism that education is no longer a luxury. Education in this day and age is a necessity."

—President Lyndon B. Johnson, "Remarks on Signing the Higher Education Act of 1965," November 8, 1965

President Johnson signs the Higher
Education Act on November 8, 1965

The Higher Education Act

First Lady "Lady Bird" Johnson and ACE President Robert H. Atwell on the 25th anniversary of the Higher Education Act, 1990.

On January 12, 1965, President Lyndon B. Johnson sent a special message to Congress, asserting that "higher education is no longer a luxury, but a necessity." Just 11 months later, on November 8, 1965, he signed the Higher Education Act (HEA) into law "to strengthen the educational resources of our colleges and universities and to provide financial assistance for students in postsecondary and higher education."

Part of Johnson's vision of the United States as the Great Society, the act authorized a variety of federal aid programs for higher education. Titles II and III of the HEA provided federal funds directly to colleges and universities and targeted support for specific goals, such as teacher preparation. Title IV authorized major student aid programs, including grants, loans, and work-study programs. To this day, these programs are the primary source of direct federal support to students pursuing postsecondary education. Additionally, the HEA authorized services and support for lower-income students (via select Title IV programs), as well as for students pursuing and institutions offering certain graduate and professional degrees (via Title VII).

When President Johnson signed the bill, he said, "For the individual, education is the path to achievement and fulfillment; for the nation, it is a path to a society that is not only free but civilized; and for the world, it is the path to peace—for it is education that places reason over force."

The U.S. Department of Education estimates that today, the HEA provides "more than $120 billion in federal grants, loans, and work-study funds each year to more than 13 million students paying for college or career school."

In a 2015 article for *Time* magazine, Freeman A. Hrabowski III, president of the University of Maryland, Baltimore County, wrote, "The Higher Education Act's most enduring legacy is a framework to provide the financial support for students from low-income families to attend college. This commitment to supporting young people from all backgrounds sent a clear message that America recognized the importance of social mobility and a well-educated citizenry."

Purdue University (IN) athletes run with Senator Birch Bayh, who coauthored and introduced Title IX of the Education Amendments of 1972, circa 1970s.

Educational Equality for Women

With the onset of the Cold War and the Korean conflict in 1951, ACE convened a conference to explore "urgent questions about just how ... women could serve the defense of the nation," including military service, industrial work, and efforts in the home. More than 900 educators, government representatives, business-people, and citizens attended the Conference on Women in the Defense Decade. They concluded that the modern woman needed higher education to become "politically literate and ... conscious of her responsibilities as a citizen in a democracy."

To that end, ACE established the Commission on the Education of Women (CEW) to research and clarify issues related to women's higher education. Operating from 1953 to 1962, CEW issued two publications: *How Fare American Women?* in 1955 and *The Span of a Woman's Life and Learning* in 1960. Both challenged the traditional notion that a liberal arts or home economics track was sufficient for women pursuing a postsecondary degree. As the commission's studies circulated, campuses across the country reexamined their continuing education options for women of all ages and stages of life. By 1971, there were more than 500 programs to assist women in entering or reentering college in order to garner broader career choices and workplace options.

Meanwhile, Title IX of the Education Amendments of 1972 declared "no person in the United States shall, on the basis of sex, be excluded from participation in, be denied the benefits of, or be subject to discrimination under any educational program or activity receiving federal financial assistance." In the year following its passage, Title IX served as the impetus for ACE's creation of the Office of Women in Higher Education. The office was designed to help its members interpret legislation, eliminate discriminatory practices, and increase women's participation at all levels of higher education—from students to professors to administrators.

Due to increased member demand for services and an expanding federal footprint in higher education policy, the Council found that it had outgrown its office space. In 1969, the W. K. Kellogg Foundation awarded ACE a major grant to create the National Center for Higher Education at One Dupont Circle in Washington, DC. Today, in addition to ACE, the center houses numerous higher education associations, facilitating synergistic contact and coordination among educational organizations.

Robert Morris University (PA) Colonials women's basketball team, winners of the Pennwood West Conference Tournament in 1984.

"Women are becoming a tour de force."

—Donna Shavlik, director of ACE's Office of Women in Higher Education (1981–1997), 2012

A 1969 rendering of the ACE building at One Dupont Circle NW.

Left: Female students at Arizona State University, circa 1970; below: Donna Shavlik (second from right), director of ACE's former Office of Women in Higher Education, who helped shape the regulations implementing Title IX.

Opposite: A 1983 women's studies class at Old Dominion University—the first public institution in the Commonwealth of Virginia to create a course for women's studies.

"*Title IX ensures equality for our young people in every aspect of their education. . . . The more confident, empowered women who enter our boardrooms and courtrooms, legislatures, and hospitals, the stronger we become as a country.*"

—President Barack Obama, on the 40th anniversary of Title IX, *Newsweek*, 2012

A Focus on Women

Mary Gertrude Smith Boddie, the first African American student to graduate from East Stroudsburg University (PA), in 1904.

Support for women has been an important issue to ACE since Congress ratified the 19th Amendment to the Constitution giving women the right to vote in 1920. That year, ACE created the Committee on the Training of Women for Professional Service, which advocated women's right to work and broadened options for their education and professional advancement. In the 1950s, ACE established the Conference on Women in the Defense Decade to expand the national understanding of women's importance, responsibilities, and opportunities. The Council also initiated the Commission on the Education of Women (CEW) that decade to focus on radically expanding the options for women in higher education, allowing them greater access to courses and degrees in fields previously dominated by men. In 1964, ACE advocated for Title VII of the Civil Rights Act, which prohibited employment discrimination based on gender.

The momentum for women's rights picked up in the 1970s with the passage of Title IX of the Education Amendments of 1972, which prohibited sex discrimination in all aspects of educational programs that receive federal support. In response to Title IX, ACE created the Office of Women in Higher Education (OWHE) in 1973. OWHE not only provided guidance for on-campus compliance with Title IX legislation, but also created pipelines for women leaders to identify and advance women candidates for college and university presidencies.

Today, the ACE Women's Network connects women pursuing higher education leadership opportunities through independent networks that engage state chairs, presidential sponsors, and institutional representatives. These independent networks create programs and resources that identify, develop, encourage, advance, link, and support (IDEALS) women in higher education careers. The ACE Women's Network Executive Council supports state networks by serving as a liaison and mentor to state chairs and as a leader for network planning boards.

ACE's success in bringing promising leaders to light is evident in a number of additional programs and initiatives. These include the Council's National and

Regional Women's Leadership Forums (established for women seeking a college or university presidency, vice presidency, or major deanship) and its Moving the Needle (MTN) initiative (designed to increase the number of women in senior leadership positions in higher education). MTN harnesses the collective efforts of higher education leaders to advance women leaders, with the goal of achieving parity for women in college and university presidencies by 2030.

Margaret L. Drugovich, chair of the ACE Women's Network Executive Council beginning in 2016, identified the importance of awareness, research, and advocacy on behalf of women leaders in higher education: "I think that women and men need to understand that women do not need to be more to be equal. We don't need to be more perfect; we don't need to be more transparent or more understanding or more patient or more compassionate or more intelligent just to be equal. I think it's time for people to recognize that simply being a woman is enough or, often, more than enough to get the challenge done."

Notes regarding Title IX of the Education Amendments, 1973.

The Michigan–ACE Women's Network Women of Color Collaborative tour the Charles Wright Museum, 2012.

Emily Taylor, director of ACE's Office of Women in Higher Education, takes the podium in 1973 at the University of Kansas to speak on equal rights.

"Not a law firm in the entire city of New York bid for my employment as a lawyer when I earned my degree. Today, . . . thanks to Title VII [of the Civil Rights Act of 1964], no entry doors are barred."

—Justice Ruth Bader Ginsburg, Supreme Court nomination acceptance speech, 1993

Facilitating Strength in Higher Education

The Association of Chief Academic Officers (ACAO) was founded during ACE's Annual Meeting in 2012.

Over the years, ACE, through its convening role, has worked to enhance coordination, strengthen diversity, and expand opportunities for collaboration.

One of the Council's most important initiatives in this area was the creation of the Washington Higher Education Secretariat in 1962. This organization facilitates collaboration among chief executive officers from approximately 50 higher educational associations. Members include the American Association of Community Colleges, the Association of American Law Schools, the College Board, and the National Collegiate Athletic Association.

ACE created the Business Higher Education Forum (BHEF), comprised of academic and corporate chief executive officers, in 1978. Spearheaded by the late ACE President Jack W. Peltason, BHEF helps members to identify issues of mutual concern to the corporate and higher education communities, make recommendations for action, and then act. In 2004, BHEF became an independent organization; the ACE president continues to serve on its board.

In 1988, during the ACE Annual Meeting, presidential assistants began to share information about their roles. In response, the National Association of Presidential Assistants in Higher Education (NAPAHE) was formally organized in 1995. It continues to provide networking and professional development opportunities to those who support presidential offices.

In 2003, ACE began to convene diversity officers during a time when many such offices were still in their infancy. After receiving overwhelming interest from diversity officers across the country, ACE created the National Association of Diversity Officers in Higher Education (NADOHE) in 2006. The NADOHE network conducts research, coordinates and shares information, and establishes methods to further inclusive excellence.

One of the most recent organizations to grow out of collaboration among ACE members is the Association of Chief Academic Officers (ACAO). Various ACE-affiliated CAOs gathered at ACE's Annual Meeting in 2012 and formally organized ACAO in 2014 to share information and determine how to best respond to the changing role of the CAO in the twenty-first century. ACAO also offers opportunities for professional development and mentoring.

Chief Justice Warren E. Burger (with Judith S. Eaton, now president of the Council for Higher Education Accreditation) speaks to the Washington Higher Education Secretariat on the 200th anniversary of the adoption of the U.S. Constitution, 1987.

Opposite: Dick Gregory at the Black Power Symposium at Augustana College (IL), 1969.

Right and below: Howard Washington Thurman, a civil rights leader and a mentor to Martin Luther King Jr., with students at Tuskegee University (AL), 1950; and students at Lawrence Technological University (MI) protest the Vietnam War, 1971.

ACE Fellows Program

AMERICAN COUNCIL ON EDUCATION
ACADEMIC ADMINISTRATION INTERNSHIP F
1965-1966 INTERNS

The American Council on Education's 1965–66 academic interns—the first class in the Fellows Program.

In the mid-1960s, U.S. colleges and universities were on the brink of two decades of explosive growth. On one hand, the first wave of the baby boomer generation (76.4 million strong) was graduating from high school. On the other, passage of the Higher Education Act of 1965 guaranteed student aid for millions of students who were college bound. The ACE Fellows Program was founded that same year to serve the capacity-building needs of higher education institutions—and to ensure that existing and future leaders would be ready to take on the demographic, economic, and cultural transitions that lay ahead.

In contrast to leadership development—historically an individual, up-through-the-ranks enterprise—the ACE Fellows Program is designed to cross-pollinate ideas, experiences, approaches, and perspectives between carefully paired executives of one institution and future leaders of another. During its intensive yearlong program, future leaders receive mentorship and participate in onsite special projects, seminars, and national meetings. The goal is to groom a national network of future leaders who are committed to making higher education in the United States as successful and responsive as possible to the nation's shifting, increasingly complex needs.

One member of the inaugural group reported: "In 1965–66, as a first-of-its-kind, the stature of each Fellow was elevated. There was a curiosity about who we were, what we learned, if the methodology was transferable. We became a cadre of individuals that institutions sought, which was an institutional endorsement that it is possible to educate and train subsequent generations of leadership."

Since 1965, approximately 2,000 vice presidents, deans, department chairs, faculty, and other emerging leaders have participated in the ACE Fellows Program. Of those, more than 80 percent have served as chief executive officers, chief academic officers, vice presidents, and deans.

ACE Fellows from the class of 1973–74.

Today's program is a customized learning experience that enables participants to immerse themselves in the culture, policies, and decision-making processes of another institution, condensing years of on-the-job experience and skills development into a single year.

In a 50th anniversary survey, 98 percent of ACE Fellows agreed that the program prepared them for a senior leadership position. Audrey Bilger, an ACE Fellows Program participant during the program's golden anniversary year, reflected on its significance: "For a full year, I read, analyzed, participated in workshops, and reflected on theories about leading. All the while, because I spent much of my time in the company of outstanding leaders, I was able to witness and engage in the art of leadership."

Dancing at the 50th anniversary dinner at the ACE Annual Meeting, 2015.

PART THREE

Fostering Equity and Change

(1974–2001)

Senator Paul Simon, with ACE President Robert H. Atwell looking on, at an ACE commission meeting in March 1987.

The period from 1974 to 2001 began with the resignation of President Richard Nixon and the invention of the personal computer—and ended with the Supreme Court–decided election of George W. Bush and the September 11, 2001, terrorist attacks. In between, the economy weathered three recessions, double-digit inflation, and an energy crisis. The Internet became prominent, the U.S. population grew and diversified from 215 million (86 percent identifying as white only) to 281 million (75 percent identifying as white only), and according to a Pew Research Center report released in 2009, college enrollments increased 40 percent from almost 11 million (54 percent male) to 15 million (56 percent female).

THE STUDENT LIFE

Volume 89, Number 20 — April 29, 1975

Pomona College's (CA) newspaper, *The Student Life*, captured students protesting for the rights of African Americans at the college in 1975.

Reginald Wilson, ACE Senior Scholar Emeritus, circa 1998.

Amid these shifting racial, gender, and underserved student demographics, the American Council on Education (ACE) worked to ensure that education and leadership opportunities were equally obtainable for minorities, women, and students with disabilities. The Council also began initiatives to help students more easily transfer from two-year to four-year colleges and created civilian programs recommending college credit for work experience.

Finally, after the 9/11 attacks, ACE assisted member institutions in recovery efforts and spoke for its members on issues such as visa requirements for foreign students. And for veterans who had served post 9/11, the Council helped increase access to educational opportunities.

One-Third of a Nation

The Civil Rights Act of 1964 prohibited racial discrimination in admissions, and the Higher Education Act of 1965 made student financial aid more widely available. To ensure that students were realizing the benefits prescribed by this watershed legislation, ACE took action in a number of significant ways.

In 1981, the Council created the Office of Minorities in Higher Education (OMHE) to champion the need for diversity in higher education. One of its major functions was to gather information for an annual report summarizing its progress. After five years of troubling results, ACE convened a commission of political, business, education, and civic leaders to grapple with the decline in minority students opting for college and the alarming dropout rate among those pursuing a degree in higher education. The report, *One-Third of a Nation*, was issued by the Commission on Minority Participation in Education and American Life in 1988. It documented the waning commitment by U.S. schools, businesses, and government officials to provide equal opportunities to minority groups who would soon comprise one-third of the U.S. population.

"America is moving backward—not forward—in its efforts to achieve the full participation of minority citizens in the life and prosperity of the nation," the report stated. "In education, employment, income, health, longevity, and other basic measures of individual and social well-being, gaps persist—and in some cases, are widening—between members of minority groups and the majority population." The report challenged the nation's institutions of higher learning to strengthen efforts to recruit black, Hispanic, American Indian, and other minority students and to retain them through graduation.

Following this groundbreaking report, ACE continued to support its member institutions in advancing access and diversity. Additional publications included *Minorities on Campus: A Handbook for Enhancing Diversity* in 1989. Under ACE President Stanley O. Ikenberry's leadership, the Council also initiated the College Is Possible campaign in 1998 to bring awareness to the wide variety of scholarships, low-interest loans, and grants available to students of all academic and financial backgrounds.

Then, to address the large numbers of minority and low-income students who were beginning their postsecondary education at local, lower-priced community colleges, ACE created the National Center for Academic Achievement and Transfer (NCAAT), which identified factors affecting student transfers to four-year institutions. From 1989 to 1992, a series of NCAAT studies examined ways community college curriculums could improve content, structure, and portability to best facilitate students' pursuit of a four-year degree.

U.S. Secretary of Education Richard Riley speaks during a College Is Possible event at the New York Public Library with ACE President Stanley O. Ikenberry.

Opening Doors

In addition to supporting minority groups, ACE expanded programs that grant college credit to veterans for military training by including credit for civilians with work-related experience and training. Established in 1974, the Program on Non-Collegiate Sponsored Instruction—now known as ACE's College Credit Recommendation Service (CREDIT®)—helps students earn credit for formal vocational training that occurs outside traditional degree programs.

ACE opened doors for disabled students as well by helping to define higher education's response to Section 504 of the Rehabilitation Act of 1973, which prohibited discrimination against individuals with disabilities. For secondary education, this included discrimination in recruitment, testing, admissions, and treatment after admissions. To foster results after the legislation's delayed implementation in 1977, ACE conducted a national survey of college freshmen who self-identified as disabled and then recommended accommodations and services to its member institutions. In 2000, ACE created the Higher Education and the Handicapped Resource Center (HEATH) to serve as the national clearinghouse of information regarding technical assistance in disability access. To help campuses fulfill a desire to be more welcoming to students with disabilities, HEATH (now housed at George Washington University) created a national clearinghouse for information about services for students, published news bulletins, fact sheets, a resource dictionary, and other materials that campuses found invaluable. This effort was one of the first attempts to gather comprehensive resource tools for campus administrators.

ACE Vice President Judith S. Eaton, with ACE President Robert H. Atwell and American Association of Community Colleges President David Pierce, speaks at a press conference, 1992.

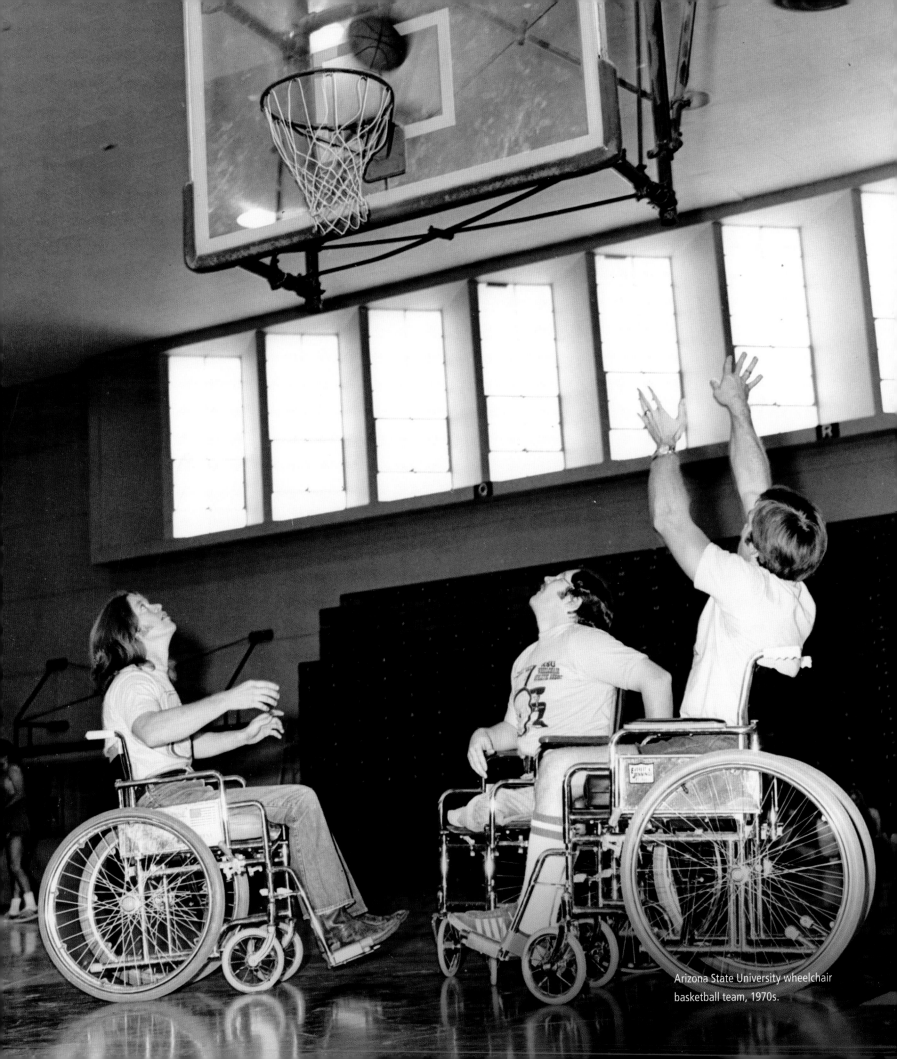

Arizona State University wheelchair basketball team, 1970s.

The U.S. Department of Education

ACE President Stanley O. Ikenberry (far right) with Richard Riley, secretary of education, and Michele Tolela Myers, president of Denison University (OH), 1997.

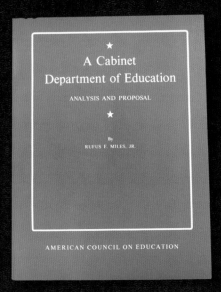

ACE's analysis and proposal for a cabinet-level Department of Education.

Although relatively new when compared to other presidential cabinet–level agencies, the Department of Education's first incarnation was in 1867, as a non-Cabinet level agency (although it was quickly downgraded and renamed the Bureau of Education and then the Office of Education). Created by President Andrew Johnson to survey schools in the United States, the department had four employees and a budget of $15,000. A year later, amid concern over federal interference in local schools, the Department of Education was placed under the purview of the Department of the Interior. The federal role in education expanded slowly in the second half of the nineteenth century and the first half of the twentieth century.

President Lyndon Johnson's 1960s War on Poverty greatly expanded federal funding for the nation's schools at all levels, from early childhood to postsecondary. The expansion continued throughout the 1970s with national efforts designed to equalize educational opportunities for underserved, minority, and first-generation students; racial minorities; women; people with disabilities; and non-English speaking students.

Reflecting its members' concern about federal intervention, ACE initially did not support President Jimmy Carter's creation of the cabinet-level Department of Education in 1979. Once the department was established, however, ACE played—and continues to play—a significant part in shaping its role and its reach in regard to higher education.

The pendulum of congressional support for the Department of Education has swung widely over the years, with most debates centered on how to reduce federal control and financial contributions to U.S. schools without giving up the goal of educational equity. Today, the Department of Education has 4,400 employees, manages annual funding of $116 billion, and holds a student loan portfolio of $1.4 trillion. Despite its growth over the past nearly 40 years, the department's mission remains the same: "to promote student achievement and preparation for global competitiveness by fostering educational excellence and ensuring equal access."

On October 17, 1979, President Jimmy Carter signed a
bill to create the U.S. Department of Education.

*"The time has passed when the federal government can
afford to give second-level, part-time attention to its
responsibilities in American education."*

—President Jimmy Carter, remarks on signing the Department of Education Organization Act into law, 1979

Diversifying Campus Leadership

Meanwhile, ACE's Office of Women in Higher Education (OWHE) set its sights on increasing the number of women in leadership positions, with special emphasis on presidencies, vice presidencies, and deanships. In 1977, after concluding that qualified women were available but overlooked, OWHE launched the National Identification Program for the Advancement of Women in Higher Education, known as ACE/NIP. Its objective was to identify talented women and enhance their visibility as leaders by holding national, state, and regional forums that addressed key leadership issues such as finance and ethics in education, the role of trustees, and importance of diversity to the educational mission. ACE/NIP was a success, as evidenced by the 225 percent increase (from 148 to 480) in women presidents at U.S. colleges and universities from 1975 to 1999.

With support from the Rockefeller Foundation, ACE further diversified the leadership pipeline by encouraging more candidates from Historically Black Colleges and Universities (HBCUs) to apply for the prestigious ACE Fellows Program. In 1982, ACE published the first of its annual status reports on minorities in higher education; five years later, the Council created the Commission on Minority Participation in Education and American Life. Today, identifying and developing college and university leaders who are representative of the general population in the United States—one that is increasingly diverse—remains one of ACE's chief strategic priorities.

Executive Challenges

As colleges and universities in the United States grappled with unprecedented change, ACE stepped forward to assist higher education presidents and chancellors in identifying and analyzing executive challenges and successful practices. In 1986, ACE

COMMISSION ON MINORITY PARTICIPATION IN EDUCATION AND AMERICAN LIFE

Dorothy Height, president of the National Council on Negro Women and member of the 40-person Commission on Minority Participation in Education and American Life, 1988.

"We're stronger when we're together . . . It's very important—very important—to try to keep the world of higher education together as much as possible."

—Robert H. Atwell, ACE President Emeritus (1984–1996)

conducted the first-ever national study to determine who these leaders were, what paths they had taken to the office, and what trends were impacting their role. ACE published the results the following year in the first edition of its American College President Study.

The study revealed that most campus leaders were white, male, in their 50s, married with children, and Protestant; held a doctorate in education; and had served six years in their current position. The majority had followed an up-through-the-ranks career path and most frequently cited chief academic officer as their prior position. In addition, most identified their biggest challenges as rapidly ballooning enrollments, escalating fiscal pressures, a wide array of constituents (including their board of directors), and a tumultuous political climate.

To assist presidents and senior leaders, ACE initiated a series of programs, services, and research. Presidential Roundtables provided daylong forums for presidents, leaders, and experts to explore pressing higher education issues. A series of workshops for presidential assistants, department chairs, and chief academic officers explored issues such as faculty bargaining, budgeting, and how to write a faculty handbook. In the late 1990s, ACE's five-year Project on Leadership and Institutional Transformation, funded by the W. K. Kellogg Foundation, invited 27 institutions to help tackle the challenging process of institutional change. Today, ACE continues to host workshops and trainings for emerging and senior leaders.

The *American College President Study 2017* reports that, despite best efforts, change has been slow. Most presidents continue to be white males in their early 60s with doctoral degrees and seven years' service in their current position. On the bright side, the percentage of women presidents has risen from 10 percent in 1986 to 30 percent in 2017, and the percentage of minority presidents is up from 8 percent in 1986 to 17 percent today.

The second edition of the American College President Study, the leading and most comprehensive study of the college presidency and the higher education leadership pipeline.

Responding to 9/11

The terrorist attacks of 9/11 affected every aspect of American life, including the higher education community. In the wake of the enormous tragedy, ACE assisted member institutions through a myriad of unpredicted issues.

The morning of David Ward's first day in the office as ACE's 11th president was spent standing alongside his new staff members watching the Pentagon burn from the windows of the Council's Dupont Circle office building. The ramifications of the unprecedented events of that day quickly consumed the first year of his tenure.

In the immediate aftermath of the attacks, ACE member institutions in New York City struggled to deal with horrific loss. One stunning example was that of ACE member Pace University, located at the center of the New York City attacks. Pace's main New York

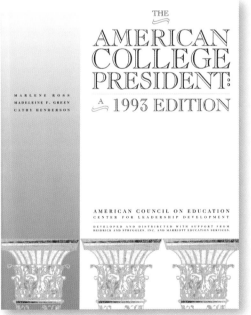

ACE President David Ward testifies before Congress on the impact of the terror attacks on higher education, 2001.

Minutes after the second plane hit the Twin Towers of the World Trade Center, September 11, 2001.

City campus occupied a number of buildings downtown, including the 55th floor in the North Tower of the World Trade Center. While those on the 55th floor were able to evacuate safely, four students and more than 40 Pace alumni working in other areas of the World Trade Center died that day.

David Caputo, president of Pace at the time, and an army of faculty and staff evacuated other on-campus students as quickly as possible. Under Caputo's leadership, the Center for Downtown New York was created to help downtown businesses secure disaster relief, and free legal services were offered by Pace's law school to victims of the terrorist attacks.

Just next door from the World Trade Center, debris destroyed the Borough of Manhattan Community College's Fiterman Hall, and six BMCC students lost their lives. The school was used as a temporary command center for rescue operations.

Many other member institutions were similarly affected by the tragedies. Students, staff, or faculty from Georgetown University (DC), Santa Clara University (CA), Northeastern University (MA), University of Maryland, University of Massachusetts Amherst, Catholic University of America (DC), University of New Hampshire, and University of California, Santa Barbara, died in the 9/11 attacks and will long be remembered by the higher education community.

Ward led the Council's efforts on a range of issues that arose after the 9/11 attacks, particularly surrounding international students and scholars. This work included advocating on behalf of member institutions before congressional panels and urging that any changes to student visa requirements carefully balance national security needs with the value that international students bring to U.S. campuses and the nation as a whole.

In an effort led by Dartmouth College's (NH) President James Wright, ACE also assisted Senator Jim Webb (D-VA) in

The Borough of Manhattan Community College's Fiterman Hall building sustained significant damage after the Twin Towers collapsed.

drafting the Post-9/11 Veterans Educational Assistance Act of 2008, which expanded higher education bene-fits to veterans of 9/11 military service and their immediate families. ACE also assisted Senator Daniel Akaka of Hawaii in drafting the Post-9/11 Veterans Educational Assistance Improvements Act of 2010, which amended and improved the 2008 legislation, including benefits for some National Guard service members. ACE pub-lished *Service Members in School: Military Veterans' Experiences in Using the Post-9/11 GI Bill and Pursuing Postsecondary Education* in 2010, which evaluated students' experiences with the 2008 legislative benefits in the first year they were available and provided recommendations for campuses to better serve students. More than 300,000 veterans and their families took advantage of benefits offered in the first year they were available.

"There is a deep sense of obligation to do what's necessary to provide an opportunity for returning veterans."

—Jim Selbe, Assistant Vice President of ACE's Center for Lifelong Learning (2001–2011), on the Post-9/11 Veterans Educational Assistance Act, *The New York Times*, 2008

Cadets are commissioned at
Saint Leo University (FL), 2013.

Post-9/11 GI Bill

Senator Jim Webb (D-VA) visiting Kadena Air Base in Okinawa, Japan, 2010.

Since the passage of the original GI Bill, ACE has provided a critical link between the U.S. Department of Defense and higher education, helping U.S. military members and veterans gain access to postsecondary learning.

In 2007, ACE assisted Senator Jim Webb (D-VA) and the Department of Veterans Affairs (VA) in crafting the most comprehensive educational benefit package yet to address the specific needs of post-9/11 veterans. In addition to supporting a range of educational options—from college classes to on-the-job training programs—ACE and the VA added two new components.

The bill, signed into law in June 2008, provided substantial support for veterans to attend any public college or university at the in-state tuition rate. It also established the innovative Yellow Ribbon program, which permitted participating private U.S. institutions of higher learning to enter into an agreement with the VA to help fund tuition and fee expenses that exceeded the amount of a veteran's GI Bill benefits. Additionally, ACE assisted the VA in creating a transfer option that enabled service members (officer or enlisted, active duty or Selected Reserve) to transfer some or all of their unused GI Bill education benefits to their spouse or dependent children. This option was only available to service members whose cumulative service was 10 years. In certain cases, however, the benefit was extended to children of armed forces members who died in the line of duty on or after September 10, 2001.

Pentagon Personnel Chief Clifford Stanley stated in 2010 that the new education benefits proved to be "a huge factor" in helping the armed forces achieve their recruiting and retention goals. But, as Keith Wilson, the VA's director of education services, added, the best measure of the program's success has been the number of students taking advantage of its benefits. In a 2010 article by the Armed Forces Press Service, Wilson said, "We have significantly more students in school, and they are pursuing their dreams. . . . At its core— that is what is successful."

Valencia College (FL) honored each of the nearly 3,000 victims of 9/11 with a flag display on the first anniversary of the terrorist attacks, 2002.

"Part of ACE's role is equipping universities and colleges in this country to be both sensitive to the crises and the targets of opportunity and enabling and supporting change and adaptation."

—Stanley O. Ikenberry, ACE President Emeritus (1996–2001)

CREDIT®: College Credit for Workforce Training

Mercedes Acuña, ACE's 2010 Adult Learner of the Year, received her bachelor of science degree in liberal arts from Excelsior College (NY) by applying work-related training courses recommended for college credit by ACE's CREDIT program.

ACE's College Credit Recommendation Service (CREDIT®) grew out of the concept that many formal workplace training courses and professional examinations might have a college credit–level equivalency and that completion might merit academic credit for nontraditional learners.

Since its establishment in 1974, CREDIT has reviewed more than 35,000 programs and emerged as the nation's leader in evaluating education and training obtained outside the classroom, including courses, exams, and apprenticeships. CREDIT reviews are performed by experienced college and university teaching faculty who embrace the philosophy that what an individual learns is more important than when, where, and how the person learned it. Review teams assess and validate each program's content, scope, and rigor. Together, the team decides whether the learning experience provides similar results to a college course. Their recommendation specifically identifies and describes the course subject, level of learning, and number of comparable credit hours that may be eligible for college transfer.

For more than 40 years, U.S. colleges and universities have trusted ACE to provide reliable course equivalency information to facilitate credit award decisions. Today, there are approximately 2,000 institutions within the ACE Credit College and University Network that recognize and consider ACE credit recommendations for workplace and military training, occupational learning, and other prior learning options. Participating organizations range from corporations, professional and volunteer associations, schools, and training suppliers, to labor unions, every branch of the U.S. military, and myriad government agencies.

Tara Turley is one CREDIT success story. Turley rebounded after losing her corporate management job by joining the Charleston (WV) Electrical Apprenticeship Program. She used CREDIT to gain college credit for many of her apprenticeship courses, and, in addition to taking classes and receiving credit from college courses taken in previous years, she earned an associate degree

Electrician Tara Turley, ACE's 2016 Student of the Year, used an apprenticeship program to earn an associate degree from BridgeValley Community and Technical College (WV).

in applied science in 2016 from BridgeValley Community and Technical College. Turley then enrolled in a multidisciplinary studies program at West Virginia University Online and was named ACE's Student of the Year in 2016.

> *"Without [CREDIT] recommendations, I may not have been able to achieve my degree."*
>
> —Kevin Burton, Maryland Army National Guard (1996–2001) and graduate of University of Maryland University College, 2015

Two students in their dorm room at Augustana College (IL), circa 1980.

Higher Education for Development

In 2006, HED partnered to train indigenous lawyers in Oaxaca, Mexico.

In 1992, ACE, along with five sponsoring associations, entered into a cooperative agreement with the U.S. Agency for International Development (USAID) and the U.S. State Department to engage higher education in worldwide development issues. Together, ACE and the American Association of Community Colleges, the American Association of State Colleges and Universities, the Association of American Universities, the Association of Public and Land-grant Universities, and the National Association of Independent Colleges and Universities founded the Association Liaison Office for University Cooperation in Development, renamed Higher Education for Development (HED).

HED's goal was to partner U.S. colleges and universities with institutions of higher education in developing countries. The partnerships sought to improve lives in host countries through collaborative research, training, educational programs, and community outreach. From faculty members jointly establishing a solar technology degree program in Jordan to students forming their own accounting firm in Kosovo, HED became an engine of social and economic change.

HED supported more than 350 higher education partnerships in 61 countries involving 140 U.S. colleges and universities from 1992 through 2015. Funding for HED partnerships came primarily from USAID and the U.S. Department of State to help educate future leaders and practitioners in a wide range of issues, including health, law, women's leadership, education, business, environment, agriculture, democracy, and workforce development.

For instance, in Laos, a HED partnership between Case Western Reserve University, the National University of Laos, and Khon Kaen University (Thailand) trained medical personnel in pediatrics and internal medicine. The number

of pediatricians in Laos rose from seven to 42 from 1997 to 2008. In another success story, Worcester Polytechnic Institute partnered with the Polytechnic of Namibia (now Namibia University of Science and Technology) to develop an affordable, community-level erosion control system. The students implemented the system in a community in Namibia and educated community members on erosion control. In South Africa, the State University of New York at Buffalo joined with the University of KwaZulu-Natal to train secondary school math instructors to teach math in grades 10 to 12, which had not been taught in 20 percent of schools prior to the program due to a lack of qualified instructors. An estimated 400 teachers were trained through the initiative.

Collaborative efforts to assist youth in central Mindanao, the Philippines, in 2012.

Terry W. Hartle, ACE's senior vice president for government and public affairs and chair of HED's advisory board, reflected on HED's educational sphere of influence. "Through their engagement abroad," he said, "U.S. colleges and universities help emerging nations develop and bank the social capital that is imperative for nation building and for the evolution and continuity of civil society."

Graduates of Ethiopia's Bahir Dar University receive HED-administered grants, 2010.

Students carry flags in an international parade at Saint Louis University (MO).

Kennesaw State University's (GA) globe statue was installed in 1996 to represent the campus's international component.

PART FOUR

Advocacy, Access, and Internationalization

(2002-2018)

Higher education faced both rapid changes and significant challenges in the aftermath of the 9/11 attacks, U.S. military engagements abroad, and the Great Recession. It also encountered a more demanding and diverse population of learners while grappling with mounting financial pressures to do more with less government and private support.

West Virginia University's iconic bell was part of the U.S.S. *West Virginia*, which was damaged during the attack on Pearl Harbor on December 7, 1941.

University System of Maryland Chancellor William E. Kirwan and Vanderbilt University (TN) Chancellor Nicholas S. Zeppos, co-chairs of the Task Force on Federal Regulation of Higher Education, testify before the U.S. Senate Committee on Health, Education, Labor, and Pensions, 2015.

Through these challenges, the American Council on Education (ACE) supported its nearly 2,000 members on a number of key fronts. ACE continued advocating the importance of a diverse campus; easing the path to a degree for post-traditional students, minorities, women, military personnel, and veterans; and enlarging the higher education leadership pipeline to include underrepresented groups. It expanded its focus in other ways too, identifying tools to ensure that twenty-first-century graduates would achieve both the cultural competency and international perspective needed to succeed in the global future.

Championing Higher Education in Congress and the U.S. Supreme Court

Congress and the White House have sought ACE's input through the years on many higher education issues such as federal financial aid, scientific research, and tax reform. For example, the Higher Education Act, which originally passed in 1965, is periodically reassessed, rewritten, and reauthorized by Congress. In advance of the 2008 reauthorization, the Council provided lawmakers with detailed research and an in-depth analysis of the proposed reauthorization provisions. ACE contributed regulatory language about the act's college cost-related disclosures and reporting, accountability and accreditation, on-campus compliance and reporting requirements, student loan "sunshine" provisions, grants for faculty professional development, international education, and future federally required studies. Once the act passed, ACE offered members summaries on all significant public policy issues and changes. The Council played a similar role in the passage of the new Post-9/11 GI Bill that same year.

In 2013, ACE President Molly Corbett Broad, along with 15 other higher education leaders, was invited by a bipartisan

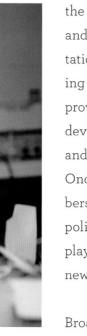

In the lab at Bronx Community College (NY), 2015.

group of U.S. senators to be a part of the Task Force on Federal Regulation of Higher Education. William E. Kirwan, then chancellor of the ACE member University System of Maryland, and Nicholas S. Zeppos, chancellor of ACE member Vanderbilt University, were asked to co-chair the task force, while ACE was requested to provide staff support. The culminating report, *Recalibrating Regulation of Colleges and Universities*, gave a wide range of specific suggestions to consolidate, streamline, and reform regulations and to improve costs and benefits to taxpayers, institutions, and students.

ACE has filed more than 200 *amicus curiae* (friend of the court) briefs over the years. Among them are submissions in 2003 to the U.S. Supreme Court in the University of Michigan's *Grutter v. Bollinger* case, and in 2013 and 2015 in the Court's two reviews of lower court rulings in *Fisher v. University of Texas at Austin*. In each case, the Supreme Court upheld the existing admissions policy. The *Fisher II* decision was "the fourth time in four decades that the Supreme Court squarely upheld this vital principle," said Broad after the Court's ruling in 2016. "This ruling safeguards an important means of achieving the diverse educational tableau needed in order to forge a challenging academic environment that produces students well-equipped to flourish in today's complex and global society."

Today, ACE continues to organize and lead *amicus curiae* briefing efforts for the higher education

Solidarity After Hurricane Katrina

Tulane University (LA) students participate in post-Katrina cleanup, 2005.

After Hurricanes Katrina and Rita devastated the Gulf Coast in 2005, ACE stepped up to assist its member institutions with both short-term and long-term response efforts. ACE served numerous members along the path of destruction, including Delgado Community College, Dillard University, Loyola University, Tulane University, the University of New Orleans, and Xavier University. Their reports of damage were universal and grim: power outages, limited means of communication, and flooding from several inches to several feet. Much of the surrounding city was experiencing the same challenges, making immediate relief virtually unattainable.

Tulane President Scott Cowen despaired over the need to cancel the 2005 fall semester, relocate students, and find a way to fix what would turn out to be hundreds of millions of dollars in storm damage. Bigger still were his concerns that he would fail to bring the university back to its former state. In a June 2014 *Times–Picayune* article, Cowen recalled a conversation with his wife in the days after Hurricane Katrina. "I'm not going to be able to do what needs to be done," he said, echoing a concern of many affected institutions. "This university has been in existence for 171 years, and I will be the one to let it down."

Immediately, ACE responded to the need to relocate students from New Orleans-area colleges and universities by urging its members to absorb displaced students into their campus communities. Nearly 500 universities nationwide responded to the Council's request, and many colleges and universities opened their doors at no charge to students. In an interview with ABC News, ACE Senior Vice President Terry W. Hartle said, "All [students] need to do is pick up a phone and call the school they're interested in attending. Schools are bending over backward for this. If there's a space available and the student is academically qualified, the schools are basically accepting the students."

In addition, ACE and the National Association of College and University Business Officers set up CampusRelief.org, a website that focused on finding solutions unique to campus communities. (In one success story, a Tulane researcher was able to connect with a lab at Northwestern University to transfer

Trash bags and debris line the front of Newcomb Hall at Tulane University (LA), 2005.

study samples for safekeeping.) ACE also worked with members to ensure they obtained disaster relief and assistance over the long term.

Cowen commented on the coordination of higher education following Katrina in the January 2007 edition of *Currents* magazine, a publication of the Council for Advancement and Support of Education. "The higher education community has coalesced more than ever before," he said. "Everyone was working to keep the mission and constituents first."

A graduate at Slippery Rock University (PA), 2015.

Binghamton University (NY) commencement, 2015.

community and monitors a wide range of legal issues that impact campuses, including diversity and inclusion, campus sexual violence, research and patents, employment law, free speech, and campus security. The Council also issues memos and white papers for ACE members addressing current legal concerns.

Frontline Strategies for Equitable Access and Diversity

Throughout its history, ACE has identified, researched, and reported trends in the nation's evolving higher education landscape and changing demography. In addition, the Council has explored public policies and promoted institutional strategies for responsive as well as proactive change and reform.

When ACE was founded in 1918, roughly 2 percent of America's 18- to 24-year-olds were enrolled in college. As a group, they were predominantly affluent white males. Approximately 100 years later, student demographics have significantly changed: according to the National Center for Education Statistics, in 2016, more than 40 percent of all 18- to 24-year-olds—approximately 12 million people—were college students, and another 8.2 million students were 25 years old or older. Of those attending college, 57 percent were female, 16.5 percent were Hispanic, and 14.5 percent were black.

These statistical shifts cannot be solely attributed to changes in the U.S. population. They reflect a significant change in the national understanding of higher education as the means to greater social, economic, personal, and civic fulfillment. Further, they demonstrate that higher education's decades-long efforts to broaden educational equity and access are succeeding, though much work still remains to be done.

ACE has helped spearhead a number of successful initiatives during the twenty-first century to broaden postsecondary diversity and access among key previously underrepresented audiences. After implementing Solutions for Our Future, a three-year campaign about the importance of higher education in society, ACE worked with the Ad Council and the Lumina Foundation to create 2007's KnowHow2Go, a program designed to help

in pursuit of educational excellence. They must prepare students who will have to navigate a nation more diverse, and a world more interconnected, than ever before."

—American Council on Education, amicus brief submitted to the U.S. Supreme Court in *Fisher v. University of Texas at Austin*, 2015

"The era of standardized mass higher education is over, and all institutions face the need to define a specific, niche mission that is responsive to some but not all of the divers

Opposite: Wittenburg University (OH) kissing bridge, a gift from the classes of 1996 and 1997. Tradition has it that couples who kiss on the bridge three times will be married.

Left: Iowa State University is known as one of the top women's basketball programs in the country, having the best conference tournament record in the Big 12. Below: Students relax outside in Holton Quad at DePauw University (IN), 2016.

low-income, first-generation middle school students prepare for college. In 2011, ACE launched the American College Application Campaign, a national initiative (conducted state by state) to assist low-income, first-generation high school seniors to complete and submit at least one college application. That same year, ACE helped convene the National Commission on Higher Education Attainment to greatly improve college student retention and degree completion.

Reaching Nontraditional Adult Learners and Military Veterans

From its first programs for veterans returning from World War II, ACE has led the national movement to promote adult-learner programs in higher education. Over time, the perception of college has shifted from being a young person's pursuit to a philosophy of lifelong learning.

ACE demonstrated its continued commitment to adult learning in the twenty-first century by expanding existing programs such as GED®, which tests for high school equivalency, and CREDIT®, which grants academic credit for workplace learning or military training. Additionally, ACE helped craft the Post-9/11 Veterans

ACE's Alternative Credit Project benefits distance students such as Theresa Shouse from East Carolina University. The program eases the path for nontraditional learners through an agreement to accept transfer credits for more general education courses.

Educational Assistance Act of 2008. The Council also helped pioneer a wide range of new initiatives. Among these programs were innovative web portals and navigation tools tailored to older students as well as the creation of alternative pathways to college credit, including 2013's Presidential Innovation Lab and 2014's Alternative Credit Project.

To address the needs of adults 65 years and older, ACE initiated a two-year study that culminated in a 2007 report titled *Reinvesting in the Third Age: Older Adults and Higher Education*. Funded by the MetLife Foundation, the study examined the lifelong learning motivations, expectations, and needs of older adults to broaden their engagement in postsecondary education.

Senator Chuck Hagel speaks with student veterans at the Serving Those Who Serve summit, 2008.

ACE continued its support of military veterans, too. With donations from private contributors, the Council began a seven-year effort in 2007 to provide academic support to more than 750 severely injured service members through a program called Severely Injured Military Veterans: Fulfilling Their Dreams (SIMV). SIMV provided support services to service members, veterans, and their family members during their recovery at Walter Reed National Military Medical Center in Bethesda, Maryland.

After the success of SIMV, ACE hosted the Service Member and Veteran Academic Advising Summit in 2014 and 2016. The 2016 summit assembled 150 experts in military-connected student populations, admissions and academic advising, veteran employment, and transition assistance. The summit enabled experts to identify, examine, and take action on how to best assist these service members transitioning from the military into education and civilian employment.

In October 2015, ACE received renewed financial support from Defense Activity for Non-Traditional Education Support (DANTES), a Department of Defense agency, to expand its capacity for evaluating military courses and occupations. DANTES helps service members and veterans pursue an education and earn degrees or certifications both during and after their military service.

The American College Application Campaign (ACAC)

Southern Utah University President Scott Wyatt with a high school student at 2016's Utah College Application Month.

In November 2005, Jordan-Matthews High School in Siler City, North Carolina, hosted an event called College Application Day, with the goal of having every senior complete and submit at least one college application form. The program was so successful that it soon spread statewide, reaching underserved students, especially first-generation students and students from low-income families. On average, 72 percent of participants enrolled in college the next fall. By 2011, ACE President Molly Corbett Broad advocated scaling the program nationwide, state by state.

Now an initiative in all 50 states plus the District of Columbia, the American College Application Campaign (ACAC) helps coordinate college application programs each fall. During the 2016 initiative, 5,727 high schools across the country hosted college application programs, resulting in 440,852 seniors submitting 744,090 college applications.

Utah Governor Gary Herbert declared November 2016 to be "Utah College Application Month." In support of the statewide initiative, Southern Utah University President Scott L. Wyatt joined hundreds of high school students at SUCCESS Academy, Canyon View High School, and Cedar High School throughout the month to talk about the advantages of attending college. Wyatt stressed that the decisions students make in high school determine the life they will lead. "There are fewer jobs and opportunities for people who only have a diploma; any education beyond high school is valuable," Wyatt said in a letter on SUU's News web page. "There are a million reasons why you should go to college, but bottom line, you will earn more money, live longer, and be a happier, healthier person."

Kyler Krause, a senior at Cedar High School, remarked, "President Wyatt's presentation made me feel like I can have a good future by jumping into my education."

Orange High School students at the first National Application and Success Campaign, 2016.

Students outside the historic Samuel Cupples House at Saint Louis University (MO). The house serves as a museum for the university's pre-1919 fine and decorative art collection.

ACE's Moving the Needle lapel pin.

Gender Parity in Higher Education Leadership

Continuing the work it began in the 1950s, ACE addressed female diversity during the twenty-first century, working with national and regional women's leadership forums. In 2012, the ACE Women's Network Executive Council and ACE's Inclusive Excellence Group convened more than 30 representatives from a variety of institutions and associations to discuss the gap between the percentage of female graduates (a 59 percent majority of all degrees) and the percentage of female higher education executives (just 26 percent of all college presidencies at the time).

The result was the 2016 launch of the Moving the Needle initiative. This initiative outlines a long-term plan to advance women in higher education leadership and achieve gender parity, with 50 percent women at senior-level, decision-making, and policymaking levels by 2030.

ACE Fellow Jean Dowdall (second from left) joins panelists Trudi Blair, senior consultant, Association of Governing Boards of Universities and Colleges; Andrea Warren Hamos, vice president, Academic Search, Inc.; and Robert Templin, former president of Northern Virginia Community College, in discussing leadership in higher education at a Moving the Needle event, 2017.

"*What institutions need to do once they have [a diverse student body] is create a learning environment that both celebrates the diversity and integrates the [educational learning that difference provides] in a very purposeful way.*"

—Lorelle L. Espinosa, Assistant Vice President of ACE's Center for Policy Research and Strategy, 2016

Portia Shields, the first female CEO and CAO of Concordia College (AL) and first female president of Tennessee State University, speaks at the Women Presidents Summit in 2008.

Undergraduate Admissions and Diversity Strategies

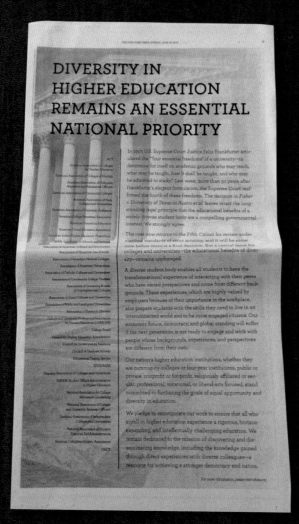

2015 *New York Times* advertisement on *Fisher v. University of Texas at Austin*, signed by ACE and dozens of associations of higher learning.

Achieving equitable postsecondary access for communities of color has been a critical goal for higher education since the passage of the Civil Rights Act in 1964 and the Higher Education Act in 1965. However, contemporary admissions policies in support of this goal have faced numerous legal challenges, namely challenges to race-conscious admissions practices. In five different decisions over the past four decades—most recently in 2016's *Fisher v. University of Texas at Austin*—the United States Supreme Court has held in favor of the holistic consideration of race and ethnicity in college admissions as one of many factors, affirming the argument and research that shows student body diversity bestows myriad educational benefits.

In response to the need for greater understanding of diversity in undergraduate admissions, ACE's Center for Policy Research and Strategy (CPRS) published a groundbreaking study in 2015 called *Race, Class, and College Access: Achieving Diversity in a Shifting Legal Landscape*. The study reflected practices by admissions and enrollment management offices at 338 institutions enrolling 2.7 million students nationally.

Coauthored by ACE, Pearson's Center for College & Career Readiness, and the Civil Rights Project at the University of California, Los Angeles (UCLA), the report examined contemporary admissions practices at four-year colleges and universities across a wide range of selectivity. "Diversity matters to higher education institutions. It matters across sectors, selectivity ranges, and university contexts. Our data are clear on that point," said Matthew Gaertner, then senior research scientist at Pearson's Center for College & Career Readiness.

One key finding of the report was that the most widely used diversity strategies receive the least attention. Gaertner explained, "Strategies such as reduced emphasis on legacy admissions, test-optional admissions, and percentage plans are the least widely used yet receive the most media and research attention. More common strategies include targeted outreach and recruitment to minority, low-income, and community college students, yet these do not receive equal press or research attention."

The report also found that striving for racial/ethnic diversity is not an either/or but a both/and proposition. Institutions that consider race in admissions decisions use other race-conscious and race-neutral diversity strategies more often and find them more effective than institutions that use race-neutral strategies alone. Some of the most widely used and effective diversity strategies at institutions that consider race include targeted recruitment and yield initiatives for minority and low-income students, summer enrichment programs, and targeted financial aid awards.

Finally, the researchers discovered that institutional reactions to the U.S. Supreme Court's decisions are evolving. Although admissions offices had made modest changes after the first *Fisher* ruling in how they approach enrollment data, admissions factors, and diversity strategies, some institutions had placed increased importance on the recruitment of community college transfers and students from low-income backgrounds. This was especially true for institutions in states that had banned the consideration of race in admissions, which supersedes Supreme Court rulings.

"One of the challenges for American higher education in the wake of the *Fisher* decision has been the lack of effective exchange of research, data, and plans," said Gary Orfield, distinguished professor and codirector of the Civil Rights Project at UCLA. "Advancing equal educational opportunity requires sharing lessons learned in pursuit of promising diversity strategies. The story of affirmative action law and policy is still unfolding and researchers must respond to the needs of institutions."

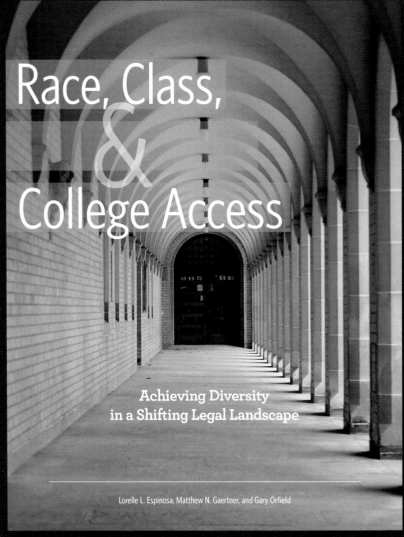

Race, Class, & College Access

Achieving Diversity in a Shifting Legal Landscape

Lorelle L. Espinosa, Matthew N. Gaertner, and Gary Orfield

ACE's 2015 groundbreaking study on how legal challenges to race-conscious admissions are influencing contemporary admissions practices at selective colleges and universities around the country.

In 2008, Benedictine University (IL) was among six institutions to receive an award from ACE for creating flexible career paths for students.

"As presidents, we must offer our sponsorship and mentorship and recognize that every presidential vacancy is an opportunity to advance women," said ACE President Molly Corbett Broad of the Moving the Needle initiative. "The presidents that have already signed on have sent a powerful signal about the importance of this issue and this campaign."

According to a 2013 Pew Research study, 51 percent of women (compared to just 16 percent of men) say that being a working parent makes it more difficult to advance in a career or a job. ACE has long recognized this struggle for women and, in 2003, began a multiyear project focused on faculty career flexibility, with support from the Alfred P. Sloan Foundation. These projects focused on research and recommendations for recruiting and retaining highly talented, diverse faculty by offering flexible career practices—an attractive benefit not only for professionals raising young children but also for those caring for aging parents. The projects have awarded grants to higher education institutions that implement flexible career practices.

Internationalization and Global Engagement

ACE has long been an advocate for the internationalization of higher education and for the global education of all students. To prepare students for the global era, more than half of the nation's colleges and universities have also embraced internationalization as an institutional priority. To complement this trend, the Council has created various initiatives, such as Global Learning for All, At Home in the World, the Internationalization Collaborative, and the Internationalization Network for Presidents and Provosts.

"Internationalization is not a frill or an add-on to the college experience; it is central to a quality education. ACE is committed to ensuring that the international dimensions of higher education are at the core of the enterprise."

—Madeleine F. Green, ACE Vice President for International and Institutional Initiatives (2001–2010)

ACE's valuable role as an advocate was affirmed in 2011 when a Blue Ribbon Panel on Global Engagement, made up of college presidents and other thought leaders, reviewed its international programming and strategy. In the panel's report, the group strongly endorsed the model of comprehensive internationalization, a concept that ACE had originally developed. This model encourages institutions to take an integrated approach to international strategy, looking beyond study abroad and international students to embrace curriculum, research, faculty development, and partnerships. The report led ACE to re-envision its international efforts, resulting in the creation of the Center for Internationalization and Global Engagement (CIGE). All of CIGE's programs—including conferences, institutions, workshops, and webinars—are designed around this model.

CIGE includes a growing research agenda that provides data and analysis to institutional leaders, policymakers, and practitioners. First published in 2003, CIGE's *Mapping Internationalization on U.S. Campuses* is the only national study that addresses all aspects of comprehensive internationalization on ACE's member campuses.

International students at Western Michigan University's homecoming.

In addition to serving U.S. institutions, ACE participates in several international forums, facilitating the exchange of policies and practices with various counterpart associations worldwide. These partnerships have ultimately expanded the capacity of higher education in developing countries. A growing number of programs promoting internationalization in the United States also include participants from other countries.

Robin Matross Helms, director of CIGE, notes the importance of globalization in higher education: "We owe it to our students—all 100 percent of them—to make sure that international perspectives and knowledge are infused throughout their educational experience from start to finish, on-campus and beyond."

❖

Dartmouth College (NH) President Emeritus James Wright.

Severely Injured Military Veterans: Fulfilling Their Dreams (SIMV)

Wounded Army veteran Sergeant Wasim Khan sought support from ACE and Georgetown's Center for Peace and Security Studies to pursue a graduate degree in international studies. Khan was a guest of President George W. Bush at the State of the Union address in 2006.

Because of advanced equipment and improved field hospitals, the numbers of wounded and disabled veterans returning from military service—versus those dying in combat—are unprecedented. While many of the wounded suffer from physical war injuries, others experience an expanded list of service-related disabilities, including traumatic brain injury and post-traumatic stress disorder.

ACE has been committed to helping its member institutions meet the educational needs of U.S. military veterans since 1944. ACE's Veterans' Programs, a nine-year endeavor that ran from 2007 to 2016, created replicable initiatives to help the higher education community expand their programs and services for veteran students and their families. One such program was Severely Injured Military Veterans: Fulfilling Their Dreams (SIMV). In 2007, James Wright, then president of Dartmouth, and Walter Reed National Military Medical Center requested academic assistance for over 700 severely injured service members. ACE responded by creating SIMV, a replicable advising model that could eventually be transitioned to other stakeholders.

In an article about SIMV published by Dartmouth in 2007, Wright said, "I found the women and men I met to be ambitious, dedicated, and capable of meeting the world's challenges, but they faced the large obstacle of completing their own education first." SIMV identified ways to meet the academic needs of this unique student population, including tutoring, career counseling, individualized education plans, support with test preparation, individual advocacy, and guidance on the college application process. It also recommended continuing academic counseling, creating spaces on campuses for veterans programs and social support, and supporting their transition to employment.

SIMV's onsite program expanded to three other military hospitals: Walter Reed Army Hospital in Washington, DC; Naval Medical Center San Diego; and Brooke Army Medical Center in San Antonio, Texas. ACE also hosted two successive Service Member and Veteran Academic Advising Summits to share their SIMV findings and practices with the larger higher education community.

View from the University of Arizona's (UA) Ina Gittings Building, named for the former faculty member from 1921–51 who founded the Women's Athletic Association and was influential in expanding opportunities for women's physical education and sports.

Internationalization Laboratory

ACE International Lab participants at West Chester University (PA).

Created in 2003, the Internationalization Laboratory (the Lab) is the cornerstone of the Center for Internationalization and Global Engagement (CIGE). The Lab guides ACE member institutions as they define and pursue their internationalization goals. To date, over 125 colleges and universities—most from the United States, with a growing contingent from other countries—have participated in the Lab.

During their 18-month engagement with the Lab, institutions develop a plan for "comprehensive internationalization," which CIGE defines as "a strategic, coordinated process that seeks to align and integrate policies, programs, and initiatives to position colleges and universities as more globally oriented and internationally connected institutions." To meet these goals, participants inventory existing activities, identify gaps and opportunities, and craft a unique plan to engage the entire campus community.

A hallmark of the Lab is its collaborative approach. In addition to receiving guidance from ACE experts, institutions benefit from learning from their peers. After completing the Lab, participants remain part of the CIGE family and are often asked to contribute to research studies and provide case examples for resources such as CIGE's Internationalization in Action series and Internationalization Toolkit. Recently, CIGE inaugurated the Lab 2.0 program, which allows previous Lab participants to revisit the internationalization plans they developed, assess progress, and make updates.

Mark A. Heckler, president of Valparaiso University (IN) and a 2010–11 Lab participant, said: "The Strategic Plan for Internationalization is the first such plan for our institution, and thus a document of practical as well as historical importance. Your process has allowed us to achieve greater maturation and cohesiveness in our thinking. Now we turn our ideas into action!"

ACE Internationalization Lab participants at the
University of North Carolina at Greensboro, 2012.

*"Our team has learned so much during the Internationalization
Laboratory process, both through the materials that we gathered
from ACE and through the deeper knowledge we have gained about
our own terrain in terms of internationalization."*

—Mark A. Heckler, President, Valparaiso University (IN), 2010–11 Lab participant

Opposite: Sunrise over Bellingham Bay at Western Washington University.

Left and below: The Lakewood Campus of Red Rocks Community College (CO); and Tufts University, overlooking Medford, Massachusetts.

Black Hills State University's (SD) main campus is located in Spearfish but students can also attend courses in Rapid City, pictured here, or Pierre.

AMERICAN COUNCIL ON EDUCATION

President Bill Clinton was among the key speakers
at ACE's 77th Annual Meeting in 1995.

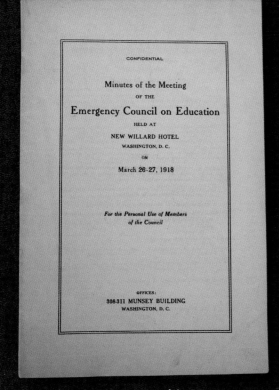

CONFIDENTIAL

Minutes of the Meeting
OF THE
Emergency Council on Education
HELD AT
NEW WILLARD HOTEL
WASHINGTON, D. C.
ON
March 26-27, 1918

For the Personal Use of Members
of the Council

OFFICES:
308-311 MUNSEY BUILDING
WASHINGTON, D. C.

Minutes from the 1918 meeting of the Emergency
Council on Education, held at the new Willard Hotel.

A session from ACE's Annual Meeting, 1973.

Except when wartime travel restrictions forced ACE to conduct its Annual Meetings via correspondence from 1942 to 1945, ACE has been convening college and university presidents and higher education leaders for its Annual Meeting every year for the past 100 years. The first Annual Meeting of the Emergency Council on Education (later renamed the American Council on Education) took place March 26–27, 1918, at the new Willard Hotel in Washington, DC. This initial meeting had fewer than two dozen attendees and was focused solely on organizing the logistics of the new organization. By its 50th anniversary, ACE counted more than 1,600 members with an Annual Meeting spanning three days and eight programmatic concurrent sessions. Today, ACE has more than 1,800 members, with its 2017 Annual Meeting featuring over 70 different programmatic and business sessions and attracting over 2,200 attendees.

According to notes on the 50th Annual Meeting in 1968, the goal of the meetings became a quest for how higher education "could serve mankind in the mass and man as an individual both responsively and responsibly." This goal still resonates today, as the Annual Meetings seek to address how institutions can become more responsive to the critical issues facing higher education and wider society and yet still maintain the continuity, stability, and relative autonomy of the academic community. Each meeting features a nationally known roster of leaders from ACE member institutions, beginning with the Robert H. Atwell Plenary, named for the distinguished former ACE president who served from 1984 to 1996. Other guest speakers have included President Bill Clinton, U.S. secretaries of education, congressional members, and renowned figures from across the academic, media, technology, and other spectrums, including Kofi Annan, Michael Beschloss, Doris Kearns Goodwin, Alan Greenspan, Reid Hoffman, Sal Khan, Robert Putnam, Condoleezza Rice, and George Will.

ACE had record attendance at its 99th Annual
Meeting in Washington, DC, in 2017.

"*As ACE heads toward its centennial year, the Council's responsibility to help campus leaders see around corners and understand how to meet constantly evolving challenges and capture corresponding opportunities has never been more important.*"

—Molly Corbett Broad, ACE President Emerita (2008–2017)

The Daniel L. Goodwin College of
Business at Benedictine University (IL.)

Opposite: The gothic-style Alumni Memorial Building at Lehigh University (PA) was built in memory of alumni who fought in World War I.

Left: The Krone Advising Center at Morningside College (IA) is specifically focused on serving the counseling needs of first-year students as they navigate college life.

Below: The Guam Community College Learning Resource Center, erected in 2010, was the first government of Guam building to be certified as LEED (Leadership in Energy and Environmental Design) Gold by the U.S. Green Building Council.

U.S. higher education has changed dramatically over the past 100 years in ways that could not have been imagined in 1918. As a community, we have faced challenges—including constrained public funding, concerns with affordability, a changing workforce, a now-global higher education marketplace—but we also have seen an encouraging and hopeful expansion of both those who attend college and those who lead our institutions. The number and kinds of higher education institutions in this country also have expanded exponentially over the century. All of these historical changes have demanded cooperation and strong leadership to forge a path ahead. ACE looks forward to many more years of working with our members and the higher education community to better serve our students and to meet the nation's education imperative to promote national competitiveness, individual opportunity, and equitable social mobility.

A graduate at Ohio University.

TIMELINE

AMERICAN COUNCIL ON EDUCATION

Donald J. Cowling
ACE President 1918–1919

Charles Riborg Mann
ACE President 1922–1934

First edition of
*American Universities
and Colleges* is
published (1928)

ACE publishes
first official listing
of accredited
higher education
institutions (1920)

1918

1925

1930

Representatives from 14
higher education associations
officially form the Emergency
Council on Education (1918)

First Annual Meeting is
held (1918)

The Emergency Council
on Education becomes
the American Council on
Education (1918)

Samuel Paul Capen
ACE President 1919–1922

ACE's Committee on the
Training of Women for
Public Service issues
research on women in the
workplace (1922)

ACE is the first educational
association to promote
standard measures of
achievement and potential
through psychological
exams (1927)

ACE organizes the American
Youth Commission during the
Great Depression (1935)

GED® test program and Military Evaluations
Program are begun (1942)

ACE President
George F. Zook
chairs the Presidential
Commission on Higher
Education (1946)

1935

1940

1945

George F. Zook
ACE President 1934–1950

ACE begins studying the
effects of racism on black
children (1938)

ACE helps draft and lobbies
for the successful passage
of the GI Bill (1944)

ACE supports
the creation of
the Fulbright
scholarship
program (1946)

UNESCO is
established (1946)

1918–1946

TIMELINE

AMERICAN COUNCIL ON EDUCATION

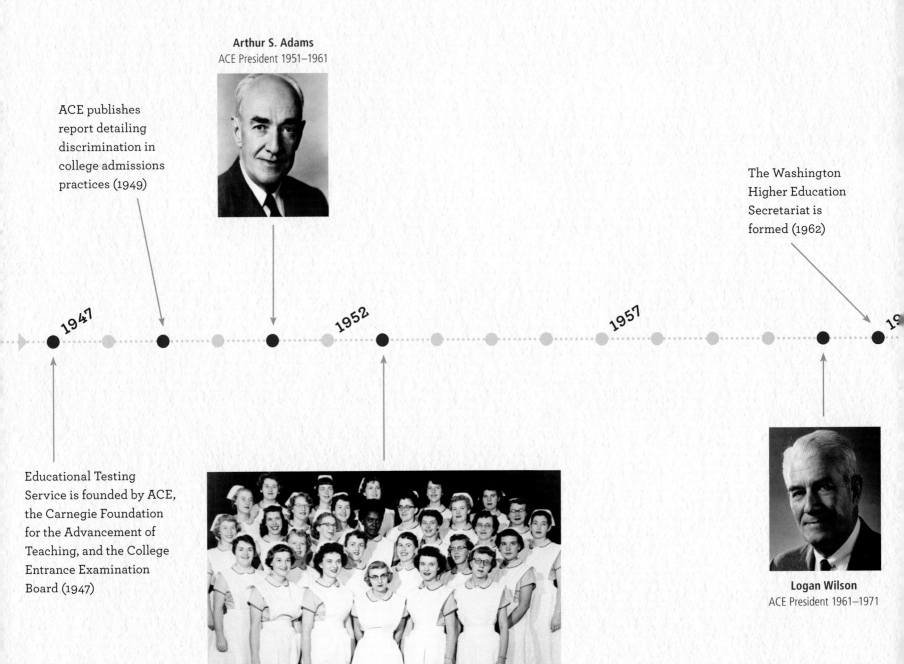

Arthur S. Adams
ACE President 1951–1961

ACE publishes report detailing discrimination in college admissions practices (1949)

The Washington Higher Education Secretariat is formed (1962)

1947

1952

1957

19

Educational Testing Service is founded by ACE, the Carnegie Foundation for the Advancement of Teaching, and the College Entrance Examination Board (1947)

Commission on the Education of Women is established (1953)

Logan Wilson
ACE President 1961–1971

Roger W. Heyns
ACE President 1972–1977

The Program on Non-Collegiate Sponsored Instruction, now known as ACE's College Credit Recommendation Service (CREDIT®), is established (1974)

The Business Higher Education Forum is created (1978)

ACE establishes the Committee on Equality of Educational Opportunity (1962) and the Office of Urban Affairs (1964)

The U.S. Department of Education is founded (1979)

Higher Education Amendments of 1972

1967

1972

1977

ACE Fellows Program is established (1965)

ACE plays a role in the development and passage of the Higher Education Act of 1965

ACE moves to the National Center for Higher Education at One Dupont Circle NW (1969)

Jack W. Peltason
ACE President 1977–1984

National Identification Program for the Advancement of Women in Higher Education (now the ACE Women's Network) is created (1977)

Office of Women in Higher Education (OWHE) is established (1973)

1947–1979

AMERICAN COUNCIL ON EDUCATION

Robert H. Atwell
ACE President 1984–1996

Office of Minorities in Higher Education is established (1981) and the first annual status report on minorities in higher education is produced (1982)

The Transatlantic Dialogues series of biennial meetings between higher education leaders in the U.S., Canada, and Europe begins (1989)

The National Center for Academic Achievement and Transfer is created (1989)

First edition of the American College President Study is published (1987)

1980

1985

1990

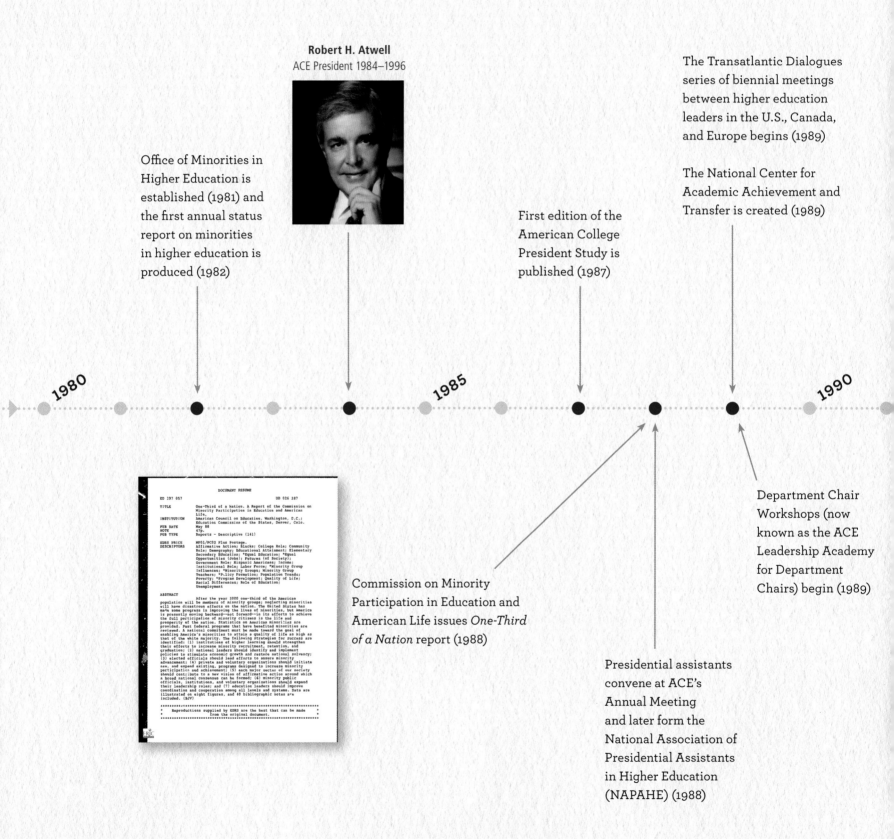

Commission on Minority Participation in Education and American Life issues *One-Third of a Nation* report (1988)

Department Chair Workshops (now known as the ACE Leadership Academy for Department Chairs) begin (1989)

Presidential assistants convene at ACE's Annual Meeting and later form the National Association of Presidential Assistants in Higher Education (NAPAHE) (1988)

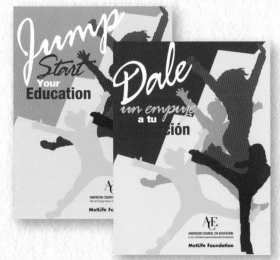

The Project on Leadership and Institutional Transformation, a five-year project on institutional change, begins (1994)

Student Aid Alliance is created by the National Association of Independent Colleges and Universities (1994)

ACE launches the College Is Possible campaign (1998)

ACE creates the Higher Education and the Handicapped Resource Center (HEATH) (2000)

David Ward
ACE President 2001–2008

1995

2000

2003

Stanley O. Ikenberry
ACE President 1996–2001

Higher Education for Development is formed (1992)

ACE begins multiyear initiative, in partnership with the Alfred P. Sloan Foundation, on advancing faculty career flexibility (2003)

First edition of *Mapping Internationalization on U.S. Campuses* is published (2003)

ACE submits amicus briefs to the U.S. Supreme Court in the University of Michigan diversity in admissions cases *Grutter v. Bollinger* and *Gratz v. Bollinger* (2003). The Council would later file briefs in support of The University of Texas at Austin in *Fisher v. University of Texas* (2013) and *Fisher II* (2016)

1980–2003

ACE helps create KnowHow2Go, a campaign to motivate low-income, first-generation middle school students to prepare for college (2007)

2004

2005

2006

2007

Solutions for Our Future, a three-year national campaign, is conducted to educate the public about the importance of higher education (2005)

ACE assists in the creation of National Association of Diversity Officers in Higher Education (NADOHE) (2006)

Reinvesting in the Third Age—Older Adults and Higher Education two-year research project begins (2007)

ACE initiates Severely Injured Military Veterans: Fulfilling Their Dreams, a program to provide academic support to service members (2007)

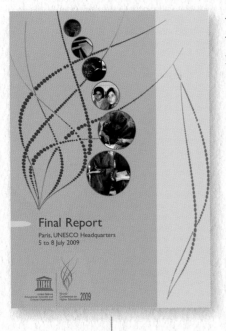

Final Report
Paris, UNESCO Headquarters
5 to 8 July 2009

UNESCO convenes the
World Conference on Higher
Education (2009)

National Commission
on Higher Education
Attainment is formed to
address college retention
and attainment (2011)

ACE and Pearson form
partnership to transform
the GED® test (2011)

Higher Education Act
is reauthorized (2008)

2008

2009

2010

2011

ACE plays a role in the
drafting and passage
of the Post-9/11 GI Bill
(2008)

Molly Corbett Broad
becomes the first
female president of
ACE (2008)

Molly Corbett Broad
ACE President 2008–2017

ACE launches the American College
Application Campaign (2010)

ACE's Center for
Internationalization and
Engagement (CIGE) is
established (2011)

ACE's Blue Ribbon Panel
on Global Engagement
issues report (2011)

2004–2011

AMERICAN COUNCIL ON EDUCATION

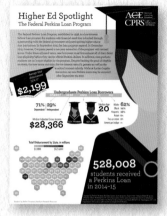

ACE's Center for Policy
Research and Strategy is
established (2013)

ACE participates in the
Task Force on Federal
Regulation of Higher
Education (2013)

Change and Innovation
Lab initiative on increasing
nontraditional student
success and attainment
takes place (2014)

ACE's National Task
Force on Institutional
Accreditation releases
report (2012)

2012

2013

2014

ACE Institute for New
Presidents is launched (2012)

CAOs convene at ACE's
Annual Meeting, leading to
the creation of the Association
of Chief Academic Officers
(ACAO) (2012)

Work takes place on
alternative pathways to
college credit, including
Evaluating MOOCs
for Credit (2012), the
Presidential Innovation Lab
(2013), and the Alternative
Credit Project (2014)

ACE-UPCEA Summit for Online Leadership and
Strategy: "MOOCs, Competency-Based Education
and the New American University" (2014)

ACE Roundtable: The Student-Athlete, Academic
Integrity, and Intercollegiate Athletics (2016)

ACE announces collaboration with the Association
of College and University Educators on online
professional development programs to advance
college instruction (2016)

Ted Mitchell
ACE President 2017–

ACE's 100th Annual
Meeting (2018)

2016

2017

2018

ACE and Strada
Education Network begin
collaboration: Examining
and Quality-Assuring Post-
Secondary Pedagogy (2016)

ACE launches the Moving
the Needle: Advancing
Women in Higher Education
Leadership initiative (2016)

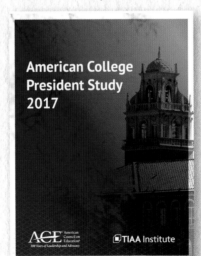

Eighth edition of the
American College
President Study is
published (2017)

Fourth edition of *Mapping
Internationalization
on U.S. Campuses* is
published (2017)

2012–2018

ACE® American Council on Education®
100 Years of Leadership and Advocacy

GREENWICH PUBLISHING

The American Council on Education (ACE), the major coordinating body and convener for all of the nation's higher education institutions, provides leadership and a unifying voice on key higher education issues and influences public policy through advocacy, research, and program initiatives.

Thanks to the following individuals for their contributions to the development of this book: Robert H. Atwell, Molly Corbett Broad, Melissa Caperton, Jeff Davies, Gailda Pitre Davis, Lorelle L. Espinosa, Jon Fansmith, Brad Farnsworth, Suzanne Forsyth, Madeleine F. Green, Kara Gwaltney, Terry W. Hartle, Barbara Hill, Stanley O. Ikenberry, Mary Beth Lakin, Lindsay Macdonald, Peter McDonough, Philip Muehlenbeck, Harold Nolte, Vanessa Resler, Philip Rogers, Michele Spires, Steven Taylor, Becky Timmons, C. T. Turner, David Ward, and Talithia Williams.

Special thanks to Sarah Zogby, who spearheaded this project and served as chief editor, and to Laurie Arnston, Ellen Babby, Ally Hammond, and Alyssa Huntley, who served as the anniversary book working group.

American Council on Education
One Dupont Circle NW
Washington, DC 20036
202-939-9300
acenet.edu

American Council on Education: Celebrating 100 Years was developed by Greenwich Publishing in cooperation with the American Council on Education. Greenwich develops and publishes custom books for leading corporations, nonprofit organizations, and colleges and universities. Greenwich Publishing is an imprint of Southwestern Publishing Group, Inc., 2451 Atrium Way, Nashville, Tennessee 37214. Southwestern Publishing Group is a wholly owned subsidiary of Southwestern/Great American, Inc., Nashville, Tennessee.

Christopher G. Capen, President, Southwestern Publishing Group
Betsy Holt, Publisher, Greenwich Publishing
Vicky Shea, Senior Art Director
Kristin Connelly, Managing Editor
Linda Brock, Proofreader
greenwichpublishing.com | 800-358-0560

ISBN: 978-1-941800-02-7
Printed in China
10 9 8 7 6 5 4 3 2 1

Photo credits are listed left to right, up and down:
Alma College (MI): 18; American Council on Education, Washington, DC: 20b, 27a, 33, 37, 47, 51, 59b, 62, 66, 67a, 67b, 68, 70, 71, 72, 74a, 74b, 76, 77, 84, 88, 89a, 89b, 103, 108a, 108b, 109, 110, 111, 124, 126–127, 134a, 134b, 134c, 135c, 136a, 136c, 137a, 137b, 137d, 138a, 138b, 139a, 139c, 139d, 139e, 140a, 140b, 141a, 141b, 141c, 142a, 143b, 143c; American Council on Education archival collection at the Hoover Institution Archives, Stanford, CA: 13, 14, 24a, 44–45, 46a, 46b, 54–55, 56b, 59a, 63, 125a, 125b; Archives & Special Collections, Vassar College (NY) Libraries: 10–11, 21; Benedictine University (IL): 112, 128–129; Binghamton University (NY): 98b; Black Hills State University—Rapid City (SD): 122–123; Bronx Community College (NY): 94b; C-SPAN: 78a; Charles Conley Photograph Collection, University Archives at Arizona State University: 56a, 73; Dartmouth College (NH): 114; DePauw University (IN): 101b; East Carolina University (NC) News and Communication photo by Cliff Hollis: 102; East Stroudsburg University (PA): 58; Findlay College (OH): 31a; Francis Falkenbury for Sarah Lawrence College (NY): 26; Franklin D. Roosevelt Presidential Library and Museum: 36b; George Mason University (VA): 8–9; Georgia State University: 4; Grove City College (PA): 38–39; Guam Community College: 131b; Dan Howell / Shutterstock.com: 78b; Iowa State University: 101a; Jimmy Carter Library: 75; jtownww2.blogspot.com: 32b; Kennesaw State University (GA): 92; Kenneth Spencer Research Library, University of Kansas: 60–61; Lafayette Studios photographs: 1940s decade collection at the University of Kentucky Special Collections, Lexington, KY: 28–29; Lawrence Technological University (MI): 16–17, 65b; LBJ Library photo by Frank Wolfe: 50, 137c; Lehigh University (PA): 130; Library of Congress: 24b, 25, 32a, 41, 48, 135a; Manhattan Community College (NY): 79; Minnesota State University Moorhead: 135b, 135d; Montgomery College (MD): 43; Moraine Valley Community College (IL): 142c; Morningside College (IA): 131a; Ohio University: 2, 15, 133; Old Dominion University (VA): 57; Orange High School (CA) and the Orange Unified School District (CA): 105; Sam Owens for the *Charleston Gazette-Mail* (WV): 85; Photograph # C-D154, C-F03912, C-F05617 Augustana College photograph collection, Special Collections, Augustana College, Rock Island, Illinois: 19, 64, 86–87; Preservation and Special Collections Department, University Libraries, University of Memphis (TN): 42b; Public domain: 134d; Purdue University (IN): 52; Red Rocks Community College (CO): 121a; Roanoke College (VA): 12; Robert Morris University (PA): 22, 53; Saint Leo University (FL): 80; Saint Louis University (MO): 90–91, 106–107; Slippery Rock University (PA): 98a; Southern Utah University: 104; Special Collections, Honnold/Mudd Library of The Claremont Colleges (CA): 69; Tufts University (MA): 95, 121b; Tulane University (LA): 96, 97; Tuskegee University (AL): 65a; United States National Archives: 27b, 36a; University Archives, State University of New York at Buffalo: 20a; University Archives, Walter P. Reuther Library, Wayne State University (MI): 34–35; University of Arizona: 116–117; University of Mary Washington (VA): 6–7; University of Maryland Eastern Shore: 42a; University of Minnesota–Crookston: 139b; University of North Carolina at Greensboro: 119; University of Rochester (NY): 23; University of South Florida: 99; U.S. Air Force: 81; U.S. Army: 115; U.S. Senate: 94a; Valencia College (FL): 82–83; Virginia Union University: 142b; Weber State University (UT): 30, 136b; West Chester University (PA): 118; West Virginia University: 40, 93; Western Carolina University (NC): 49; Western Illinois University: 31b, 143a; Western Michigan University: 113; Western Washington University: 120; Wittenburg University (OH): 100